W9-BOB-179

10

# 10 Steps to Ultimate Productivity

---

*Control the chaos of everyday life, including practical examples using the Nozbe app.*

**Author**

Michael Sliwinski

**Illustrations:**

Hubert Tereszkiewicz

**DTP:**

Papercut

**Organizational support:**

Magdalena Błaszczyk

Marcin Hinz

Natalia Mialik

Jakub Niżniowski

**Translation from Polish:**

Konrad Rozbicki

**Proofreading:**

Claire Kellems

Joy Xiang

**ISBN:**

Paper version: 978-83-945086-5-4

**Copyright** © 2018 by Michael Sliwinski

ISBN 978-83-945086-5-4

9 788394 508654

# Dedication

---

*I would like to dedicate this book to the over half-a-million Nozbe users who work hard to meet their goals each and every day. We've been learning from each other about how to live a productive life and find fulfillment in what we do for over 11 years now. Thank you for your support and suggestions, and for constantly motivating me and the entire Nozbe team. Thank you for everything that you do.*

*Michael*

With this book, you will learn

# the basic rules for building your own time management system.

# Foreword

---

*In this book, you will learn the principles needed to build your very own system for organizing and taking charge of your time. In 10 easy-to-follow steps, I will share how you can quickly and easily realize your goals. Thanks to these rules, I am both happier and more productive.*

## It wasn't always this way...

By nature, I am an incurable optimist and a generally disorganized person. That is exactly why I decided to look into the literature on self-management. I knew that I could no longer neglect my deadlines, postpone my meetings, and lose my way in the flood of information and projects that I was responsible for. I needed to finally get organized!

My old way of using a physical planner was quickly becoming outdated and couldn't keep up with the new, fast-paced environment the internet had created.

Things could not continue like this for me. I was drowning in the sheer volume of things I needed to do. That's when I decided to study the techniques of self-management. Seeking inspiration from books by authors like Stephen Covey and David Allen, I hoped even a disorganized individual like myself could tidy up their life. I never imagined I would find my life's passion through this endeavor.

## It started out innocently enough

After reading a few books on productivity, I was able to organize my most pressing issues. I already knew some programming, so I created a simple application for private use that enabled me to identify my goals and prioritize them. I gradually worked on my creation, and in February 2007, I decided to show it to the world. I figured that since it helped me, maybe someone else will benefit from it.

That's how the Nozbe app came to be. Its popularity, especially in the United States, exceeded all of my expectations. Motivated by its success, I left my job at the time and decided to shift my focus onto the tool that I continue to work on to this day. I no longer work alone but with an entire team. Today's Nozbe works not only in browsers but on all mainstream platforms.

*Trivia: People often ask me where the name "Nozbe" came from. The name is actually a play on the phrase "BE Naturally OrganiZed." We*

> *decided to abbreviate the name and, after a few attempts such as "Be Oz" and "Oz Be," we finally came up with "Nozbe."*

## Popularization of the productive lifestyle

Thanks to the development of Nozbe, I was able to meet many fantastic people with whom I continued to learn new ways of organizing one's time. Together with a friend of mine, Maciek Budzich (author of the blog Mediafun in Poland), we came up with the idea of creating a magazine about productivity. I invited some of my personal gurus, as well as many experts in the fields of time management, business, and technology to work on it. That's how *Productive! Magazine* was born, which with the help of my team, I was able to publish for more than eight years in multiple languages.

## Meanwhile...

I am still studying and testing new ways of improving productivity. Seeing so many strategies that actually work, and hoping to inspire and help you organize your own goals and time, I decided to write this book.

## It's time to get organized!

The goal of this book is to help you build your own trusted productivity system. My rules of productivity are heavily embedded in Nozbe, so it will be featured in some of the examples. However, you don't need to use Nozbe to take advantage of the advice and methods in this book. If there are programs or tools you feel more comfortable with, you should by all means use them instead. Of course, I would be very happy if you decide to use my app. What's most important, though, is that you benefit from the tips mentioned in this book and are able to incorporate them into your own personalized system. Throughout the book, you will also learn about some of the other helpful tools that are available.

## How was this book conceived?

The idea of writing this book came after recording my video course, "10 Steps to Ultimate Productivity." Together with the Nozbe team, I started by making small edits to the existing script for the video course. We invited Nozbe users to help out as well, and together we created a launch team made up of 200 true productivity

aficionados. It soon became apparent that simply releas-
ing the written script from the video wouldn't be enough.
Our ambitions were far greater. In order to properly explain all of the subjects, we decided to make even more
edits to the script. Some topics that I had merely touched
upon in the video course were expanded. A book allowed
us to include related examples as well. Not all of them
came from my own experiences. Some examples were
sent in by other members of the publishing team, and
the list of everyone involved can be found at the end of
the book. I hope that the fruit of our joint labor results
in a practical guide that will allow you to easily master
all of the important techniques for increasing efficiency.

**Before we begin, let's look at three common myths about productivity!**

Although productivity has become a popular topic—for articles, blogs, and applications—many people still seem to be skeptical about it. The main sources of this skepticism are most likely these three myths that we will put to rest right here.

Three common myths about productivity

# Myth 1: Productivity is for boring people.

# Myth 2: Productivity is for rocket scientists.

# Myth 3: Productivity is for the organized.

## Myth 1: Productivity is for boring people

Are well-organized people just plain unspontaneous? No, quite the opposite! As you will discover in the first part of the book, well-organized people don't think of 10 different things at once. Because they have everything written down in their productivity system, they can focus on the present.

The fact that they don't have to constantly think about their responsibilities allows them to be more creative, more spontaneous, and enjoy life.

*Example: In 2016, I got away for a week-long vacation to Italy with my wife. We spent our time enjoying delicious breakfasts on the shores of the Mediterranean Sea, taking long walks, and sightseeing. However, in order for this kind of a trip to happen in the first place, we needed to organize all of our professional activities before going away as well as get someone to babysit our children (many thanks to my parents!), buy plane tickets, reserve adequate accommodations, arrange car rental, etc. In order to truly live in the moment and fully absorb Italy's beauty (rather than stress over being in a foreign country), we needed to get organized before the trip.*

## Myth 2: Productivity is for rocket scientists

I've heard many people complain that this whole pro-ductivity thing is some kind of rocket science—that you have to be exceptionally skilled in order to be able to sort everything out and keep organized without going mad.

No, you don't! In the upcoming sections, you will see for yourself that everything I write about simply requires some good old-fashioned common sense. The tips are easy to put into practice and don't require any scientific gizmos or a PhD. They require developing a routine and a trusted system. This book will help you get rid of bad habits and make more productive ones.

*Example: One of my employees had problems with publishing regular blog posts. She was kind of lost in the number of little steps needed to stay on top of her work. It was stressful for her and not very comfortable for the other market-ing team members. She finally took action and sat down for 30 minutes to list all the blog en-tries she would like to publish next month. Then, she looked in the calendar and assigned a date to each publication. Next, she thought of the im-ages and graphics required for every article and tasked our graphic expert with creating them. Finally, she transferred all the arrangements into*

*Nozbe by creating a new project for it. Once the month was planned out, she generated a project template to have a base for future monthly blog schedules. Everyone thought she wasn't very well organized. It wasn't that—she just hadn't organized this aspect of her work. Once we motivated her and she found some "space" to work it all out, everything went smoothly.*

## Myth 3: Productivity is for the organized

Yet another excuse that I hear too often is that only those who are naturally organized can be productive. As you already know from the introduction, I myself am a chaotic person! It's only thanks to the simple techniques that I'm going to share with you that I was able to get organized. If they worked for me, they'll work for anyone.

On the flipside, my wife is well-organized by nature. Ever since I can remember, I've envied her because it seemed like everything came to her so naturally. Yet, despite all odds, I've managed to become a worthy opponent!

In fact, recently, she herself admitted that it's hard even for a naturally organized person not to get lost without a good productivity system. There is simply too much information to absorb, which is why the tips included in this book will come in handy for both disorganized beginners who want to dig themselves out of their heaps of obligations, as well as for those who simply need a hand dealing with current affairs.

*Example:* For years, I've been struggling to set up a proper morning routine. I've heard of many people who had it figured out: they'd wake up and follow a routine that would help them get a great start to the day. I couldn't do it consistently. I was too disorganized in the morning, and because I work from home and don't have to commute to work, I got away with my morning chaos. Two years ago, I decided to change it. As cliché as it sounds, I created a checklist for things to do in the morning, and every day as I woke up I'd follow the same checklist: go the bathroom, write in journal, pray, prepare tea, get dressed. After a few months, I got the hang of it. Now I don't need a checklist anymore; I have a routine that gets me pumped up for the day!

## Productivity in 10 steps—here's what it's all about!

The book has been divided into 10 simple chapters. I approach each issue in a concise and matter-of-fact way, making sure to include practical examples.

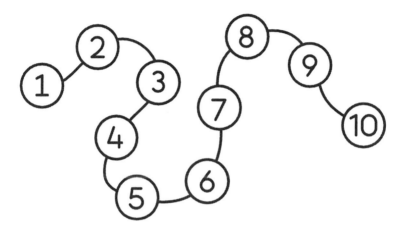

**Step 1** focuses on **clearing the mind** and moving everything you think of into a trusted system. In this part, I'll explain why it's not worth keeping all your thoughts bottled up inside your head. You'll learn how to make use of practical tools, like having boxes for incoming items—inboxes if you will—in such a way as to not forget anything, while still being able to focus on pressing issues.

**Step 2** is all about **converting commitments into projects**. It's in this section that you will find out how to break down big problems into smaller, easier steps. This will allow you to be confident that you can accomplish any goal you set for yourself. After this lesson, you will become a master at managing projects.

**Step 3** concerns **prioritizing your actions** and moving your projects forward. Properly assessing your priorities ensure the success and the smooth operation of projects. You will learn that sometimes all it takes is the smallest step (no pun intended!) for an entire project to start moving forward and bring the set goals closer.

**Step 4** pertains to **productivity, independent of time or place**. These days, work doesn't only require the use of computers, but smartphones and tablets as well. Modern technology allows us to work on-the-go and save a lot of time in the process.

**Step 5** contains everything you need to know about **working with others**. We live in an interconnected world where friends and coworkers can help you realize your objectives and reach your goals. You will learn how to share projects and communicate with others more effectively using tasks.

**Step 6** focuses on **working with categories (also known as contexts)**, which represent the second tier of grouping tasks after projects. They allow you to sort your tasks in practical ways, such as where they are carried out or the tools required for their realization.

**Step 7** deals with **managing documents and files**. Here, you will find out how to store notes and other materials to be sure that everything you need for achieving your goals is within arm's reach. I will share applications and tricks that can come in handy.

**Step 8** is dedicated to **reviewing your productivity system**. Once a week, you should meet with yourself to review your objectives, projects, lists, and goals. You will learn how to productively start each and every week!

**Step 9** focuses on the **art of managing emails**. You will see how to systematically clean out your inbox and deal with the expectations of those with whom you correspond electronically. In other words, I'll show you how to not sink in the flood of incoming messages.

**Step 10** will help you **implement everything I've taught you into your life**. I will also slip in a few more hints and tips that have worked for me and mention my favorite sources of knowledge and inspiration from the field of productivity.

The Two-Minute Rule:

# If there's a task you can do in less than two minutes, do it!

### Bonus: The Two-Minute Rule

*I'll end this introduction with a practical tip you can implement right away. Even if you don't read this book in its entirety, this trick will let you experience the magic of simple habits that help you manage your time. Allow me to introduce the Two-Minute Rule.*

*If there's something that you need to do, and you can do it in less than two minutes, do it! Seems easy, doesn't it? Here are some examples:*

- *A colleague from work sent you a message with a quick question. Answer him right now—quick and to the point.*
- *You were just notified about a meeting? Mark it in a calendar right now.*
- *Got an idea for a business? Write it down on a napkin. Don't let it slip by!*
- *Got papers lying on your desk? Do you know where they should go? Put them in an appropriate place right now.*
- *Sister's birthday? Quickly write down some well-wishes and send them right now. Don't wait until midnight.*

Try to incorporate this rule into your life, and you'll be surprised by just how many things take only two minutes. Thanks to this simple rule, you will make a habit of getting things done, rather than pushing them aside. Once you're able to deal with small things quickly and effectively, you can approach tougher and more time--consuming goals.

There is, however, one thing you must always remember about the Two-Minute Rule: don't ever tell your partner about it. Why? Because ever since I told my wife about it, she quickly figured out how to turn it against me:

- We wake up in the morning. My wife asks me to make the bed. I try to wheedle my way out of it, and of course she says, "Dear, it will only take you two minutes!"

- In the evening after dinner, my wife asks me to take out the trash. I tell her that I'll do it later. She replies, "Didn't you tell me that if something takes less than two minutes, you should never postpone it?"

Yes, this rule really does work both in your private as well as your professional life. Tweet me your own example of a two-minute task. My Twitter handle is @MSliwinski.

> **Bonus materials:** Want to be better prepared before starting the book? I've gathered a package of practical articles, templates, and videos just for this book. You can download it for free at: **ProductivityCourse.com/bonus**

In this chapter, you will learn that

# it helps to clear the mind and get all those overbearing details into your own productivity system.

# **Step 1.** Clear Your Mind

---

*How to use a trusted system to free your mind*

You think about and try to remember too many different things at once. I'm sure that you've exclaimed in the past, "I've got too much on my plate!" This is not a good thing. It's exasperating and causes anxiety. "Where have I written down the details about that meeting? Whom should I call now? Wasn't I supposed to pick up my daughter from kindergarten? Didn't I promise to give my feedback on John's presentation? How should I prepare for tomorrow's meeting? What time does it even start?"

It helps to clear the mind and get all those overbearing details into your own productivity system. This book will help you create your own system step by step. Some write their thoughts and ideas into a notepad, some use calendars, and others use a dedicated mobile application. Find out what suits you best.

My wife often jokes that I'm like an old computer with all of its default settings. I recognize only 16 basic colors, and I pretend that I'm a multitasker when in fact I only know how to do one thing at a time. Like David Allen explains in his book *Getting Things Done*, when the mind is filled with concerns, it's impossible to do any specific task. It's difficult to be efficient when your thoughts are all over the place.

## Exercise 1: Clear-your-mind activity

For this first exercise, I'd like you to write down, on one sheet of paper or on the next page, everything that's currently on your mind in whatever order it comes. Write down whatever you're thinking about—it doesn't matter whether these are trivial concerns or grand strategic goals. Write out everything, one after another, line after line. Give yourself about 15 to 30 minutes. I'm not joking. Do it now—I'll wait...

# Exercise:
## Clear your mind

Write down whatever you're thinking about—it doesn't matter whether these are trivial concerns or grand strategic goals.

Well? Was that one sheet enough? I bet that you wrote using the smallest handwriting you could manage. After doing this exercise, you may have discovered that you have too many things on your mind and it might be best to categorize your tasks..

## Embracing productivity

This is where our adventure with productivity techniques begins. You need a trusted system where you can easily store thoughts about everything you're not currently working on. This way, you will no longer need to worry about anything slipping your mind. You'll also be allowed the space necessary to work in full concentration.

## A place for your thoughts

The place to which you allocate these thoughts from your head is called an inbox. It's a "container" of sorts for all your ideas, files, documents, emails, notes, and messages. Everything that burdens your mind should go here.

The problem is that we tend to have more than one inbox—sometimes way more than one! Before I describe all of my inboxes, take a look around for yours: mailbox, email inboxes, your smartphone photo folder, Facebook Messenger, WhatsApp messages, texts, notes in your paper calendar, schedules on your phone, your desk drawer, that piece of paper on your fridge, and even that reminder scrawled with lipstick on your mirror! It's amazing how many places you keep your information stored!

## How do you deal with something like this?

The solution involves:

- limiting the number of inboxes,
- remembering the ones you actually use,
- regularly clearing all of them out.

Some inboxes are physical and others virtual. Here's a list of a few of my inboxes; you may have many more.

## The inboxes I use

**1. Email inbox** – this is the place where all my emails end up. Every day, I process my emails by reading them one by one and deciding:

- whether I can respond immediately or not (according to the Two-Minute Rule),

The inboxes I use:

**Email inbox**

1

**Physical inbox**

2

**Nozbe inbox view**

3

**Voice memos**

4

**Computer's Downloads folder**

5

- whether I feel like responding now or choose to reply at a later time (I move it to my "For Later" folder, although I try not to do it frequently),
- whether it requires additional action (in this case, I add a task in the appropriate Nozbe project),
- whether it's something that I need to save (for example, I move invoices to where they belong or print them out right away).

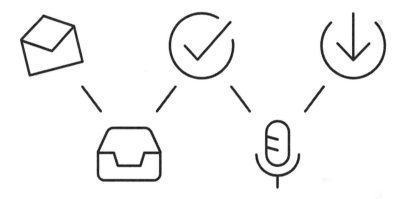

Deciding exactly what to do with each and every message is of key importance!

**Note!** *I encourage you to learn more about dealing with emails when we go into more detail later in the book.*

**2. Physical inbox** – I use a desk drawer to keep all my documents, letters, bills, and even greeting cards. At the end of each week, I go through it thoroughly and empty it. I approach it similarly to how I manage my email inbox: I open the drawer and take all the papers out one by one. For each item, I decide whether to discard it, keep it, or scan it.

**A real-life example:** *My wife once put a document on our nightstand. Although I realized that something was there, I didn't pay much attention to it and simply pushed it aside so that it wouldn't bother me during the night. I didn't even give it a second look. After a week, my wife asked me, "Honey, did you sign that document?" "What document?" I asked. "The one I put on the nightstand a week ago!" To which I answered, "Honey, you know very well that unless you put it in my drawer, I won't take care of it!" That's just how the magic of habit works; there are places I look into both regularly and thoroughly, as well as ones that I don't even pay attention to.*

Clearing my physical inbox can be exciting. Since the drawer is pretty large, I fill it with everything I know that I will need to take care of. Sometimes even packages, books, and other surprising objects end up in there.

**Tip:** *There is always a notepad and a pen next to my keyboard on my desk. When something im-*

> *portant comes to mind, I write it down immediately. This technique is especially helpful during conversations with people when ideas pop up all on their own. Sometimes I end the day with a piece of paper completely covered with notes. I then put it into my drawer and look through it later. Thanks to this, nothing ever slips my mind.*

**3. Nozbe inbox view** – Nozbe is my application for managing projects and tasks. It's here where I put any task that come to mind. At the end of each day, I sort out the mess and make decisions about what needs to be done. Maybe the task can be assigned to an already existing project. I might want to do some tasks as soon as possible, but some can be postponed. Some tasks, when I review them, don't look as good as when I first added them, and they end up in the trash.

One of the biggest advantages of Nozbe's inbox is that I always have it with me. I can add tasks to it using any of my devices—whether it's a smartphone, tablet, or a computer. I can add tasks with a quick keyboard shortcut or a couple of simple clicks. I can also automatically add a task by sending a message with its contents to my private Nozbe email address.

**4. Voice memos** – When I don't have the time to write, I take out my smartphone and click the application for recording voice memos. I dictate my thoughts and save them. I make sure to check these kinds of notes once a week as well.

I can also add tasks directly to Nozbe via Siri who can understand the due date and time of a task as well as a project and basic recurrence patterns. It works the same with Google Assistant on Android mobile devices.

**5. Computer's Downloads folder** – once a week, I empty the default folder in which I save all my downloaded data, applications, and documents, deciding what to do with each file individually. I advise saving all sources to the Downloads folder and not onto the desktop. Desktops full of files can be distracting and give the impression of having a messy computer, though a messy desktop can serve as motivation to clean it up faster!

> **Note:** *This form of inbox can be easily eliminated if you use the Two-Minute Rule when download-ing files; you've just got to make sure to save your files in their respective folders.*

So, as you see, I've got a few inboxes: my email, a phys-ical inbox, a virtual one in Nozbe, one for recorded mem-os, as well as a folder for downloaded files.

> *An example from Claire, our book launch group member and a Nozbe user: At home, I have a file*

*organizer in my kitchen that all my family's papers go into during the week. On Sundays, I empty the entire thing. I either trash, file, do, or defer each item. I don't feel stressed out during the week worrying about forgetting or losing things, because I know everything is in one spot and will get done within a week's time.*

The systematic review of inboxes is one of the pillars of operating efficiently. It is imperative that you go through them step by step, deciding what to do with each item, whether it requires two seconds of your time or much more.

I clear out some of my inboxes every day, some every other day, but I make sure to check all of them at least once a week. I realize that if I happen to not clear an inbox during the week, it will continue to worry me until I do.

# Exercise:

# Your inboxes and the strategy for managing them

Identify your physical inbox and other ones and write down, how often you are going to process each of them.

## Chapter 1 Action Plan: Clear your mind

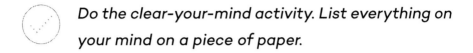

○ *Do the clear-your-mind activity. List everything on your mind on a piece of paper.*

○ *Identify your other inboxes, and eliminate all inboxes that can be incorporated into others. For example, you only need one folder for papers, one application for notes, one for tasks, etc. The fewer, the better.*

○ *Create a habit of checking your inboxes regularly. Some of them should be checked once a day, some more or less frequently depending on your preferences.*

**Good luck!**

**Bonus materials:** If you are interested in learning more about clearing your mind of worries, you can download a package of practical articles, templates, and videos about the advantages of having an inbox!
**ProductivityCourse.com/bonus**

how to achieve your goals by utilizing projects. According to David Allen, the author of *Getting Things Done*, a project is: "A desired outcome that may require more than one action step to complete."

# **Step 2.** From Tasks to Projects

*How to organize tasks in a project to bring you closer to your goal*

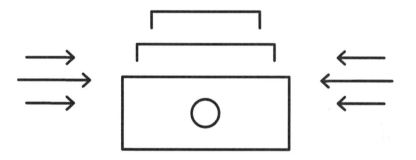

After you've cleared your mind and put everything in your inbox, you'll realize that certain items need to be handled differently. Here are a few examples of what might have appeared in your inbox:

- "Trash," which actually should be renamed to a more actionable (and probably recurring) task called "Take out the trash."
- "Brother's birthday" could either be a simple task of calling to wish your brother a happy birthday or, if

you're the one planning his birthday party, this might actually mean a bigger project.

- "Refrigerator noise" might initially mean investigating the source of the noise by calling a technician, but could turn into a whole new project: "Buy a new fridge."

As you can see, some items in your inbox might be simple actions, others can be bigger tasks, and others will turn out to be projects with a few tasks inside of them. In this chapter, you will learn all about projects and, at the end of it, you'll become a real project manager, whether you like it or not.

## Task or project?

According to David Allen, the author of *Getting Things Done*, a project is: **"A desired outcome that may require more than one action step to complete."**

For example, sharpening a pencil is a task because it requires only a single action, while gathering all the necessary supplies for a child to go back to school is a project because it involves a larger number of steps that can be spread out over a period of time.

Here are a few examples of projects that can help you understand the difference between a task and a project:

- **Brother's Birthday** – there are a number of tasks related to organizing a party for your brother's birthday. You need to invite the guests, order a cake, buy the food, decorate the room, and more depending on the type of celebration you want to have

- **Presentation for Meeting** – giving a presentation takes some preparation. This might include writing an outline, finding or creating graphics to illustrate your points, and laying out the graphics and text for each slide.
- **New Post on Blog** – publishing a new blog post includes tasks like planning the article, writing it, finding images, posting the article, and promoting it on social media.
- **Learning a New Language** – a project like this is very complex and spread over a long period of time. Each lesson is a task of its own, and the project can last many months or years, or it may not even have an actual end date. It all depends on how long you want to study and what level of linguistic knowledge you want to achieve.

## How to buy a refrigerator

Treating matters as if they were tasks when they're really projects is a common mistake. These items can seem to grow exponentially right before your eyes and quickly feel impossible to accomplish. It's no wonder that it's so hard to get them done!

This is why when I'm looking through my tasks and see one that would require more than one step to complete, I usually convert it into a project and then divide it into smaller, simpler tasks.

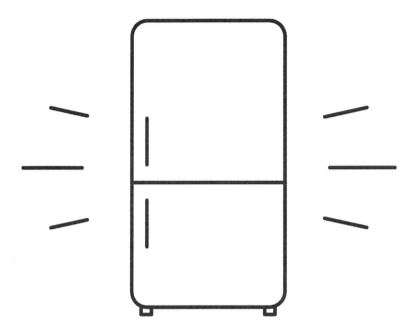

In order to better illustrate this, here's an example shared by Christopher, a member of our book launch team:

*I was once presented with what might seem like a straightforward task: buy a refrigerator. Yet I was completely overwhelmed by it. In every store, I found dozens upon dozens of them, and online I got hundreds of different options! I was finally able to complete this task once I converted the task into a project and divided it into simple stages:*

- *Choice of a brand*
- *Choice of freezer location*
- *Choice of its dimensions (mostly height)*
- *Deciding on a color*

- *Choice of four or five models in my preferred price range*
- *Deciding on key characteristics and functions (number of shelves, a big shelf for bottles, low power consumption, etc.)*
- *Choice of a final model*
- *Choice of a store with the lowest price, including delivery and pickup of old fridge*
- *Placing the order*

*Just a few days later, I became the happy owner of a brand-new fridge.*

This example proves that even seemingly trivial things like this can become problematic until we realize that they are projects and simply require the right approach.

## The art of naming your projects and tasks

As we learned earlier in this chapter, how you name projects and tasks also influences how fast things will get done. Some words push us to action or motivate us more, others less. Often, the simple change of a noun into a verb is all it takes to get you started working on a task or project.

## The name of a project should reflect its goal

For the most part, I title my projects using nouns and short descriptions of what the project's goal is. Looking back at the above examples, "Brother's Birthday," "Presentation for Meeting," and "Buying a Fridge" are good names for projects. They're simple and concise—that's all you need. Looking at them, you can't help but feel like immediately taking on the list of tasks and getting to work. Which is why...

## Titles of tasks should describe the actions we're taking

It's best to use action verbs that give a clear picture of what we actually have to accomplish. To help illustrate this theory, I'll use the example of buying a refrigerator. I'd change the activities described by Christopher in a way that makes them more dynamic. In the task "Choice of freezer location," I'd replace the words "choice of" with the more motivating "choose a," and in "Decide on a color," change "deciding" to "decide." This way, the task list in this project would go as follows:

- Choose a brand.
- Choose a freezer location.
- Choose the dimensions (mostly height).
- Decide on a color.
- Choose four or five models in my preferred price range.
- Decide on key characteristics and functions (number of shelves, a big shelf for bottles, low power consumption, etc.)
- Choose a final model.
- Choose a store with the lowest price, including delivery and pickup of old fridge.

I'd also deal with the "Brother's Birthday" project in the same way. This is how I'd phrase the tasks:

- Prepare a list of guests to invite.
- Call everyone from the guest list.
- Order a cake.
- Gather menus from five restaurants in the area.
- Decorate the room with help from my wife and my brother's wife.

Tasks written this way feel more dynamic, concrete, and precise. It really makes you want to get down to it!

I once saw someone had written for themselves a task entitled "Mom"—short and ambiguous. So I asked the person what it meant. He just made a dull face and said he wasn't exactly sure. Maybe he was supposed to call his mom. Or maybe send her his best wishes? Perhaps remind her about something? I suggested that he should try to include a verb in the title next time to make it more descriptive yet specific. "Call Mom for her 58th birthday" doesn't leave any room for doubts about what to do or why.

## How many projects should you have?

From experience, I know it's better to have more projects rather than fewer. Despite common opinion, a larger number of projects can actually make your system feel more transparent. A clear division of projects allows you to see with a glance what you've still got to do and what goals are still ahead. Busy people typically have around 30 to 50 projects, while some have up to 100 projects

A

B

C

D

E

F

G

H

I

Productivity experts recommend listing projects in alphabetical order. This allows you to easily find the desired project and access the specific tasks that it contains.

on their list. This number of projects can quickly get out of hand, which is why it's best to systematically review your project list—something you will learn more about in Chapter 8.

Experts on productivity recommend listing projects in alphabetical order, and I usually follow this rule as well. This allows me to easily find the desired project and access the specific tasks that it contains. Since I know that "Brother's Birthday" is going to be under "B," I don't have to look through the entire list; I know that it will be close to the top. However, it's up to you; you may prefer to order the projects manually and put the most urgent ones at the top of the list.

## Managing projects in practice using Nozbe

Since we've gone through the theoretical part of the chapter, now I'd like to show you how to bring this all into practice by using the Nozbe application—the tool that I use myself. Other apps for managing tasks and projects work very similarly, so what I'm about to show you should be simple to follow for users of other systems as well.

Why do I insist on using digital tools for task and project management? Because they're easily accessible. When managing projects on a piece of paper or using a calendar, you tend to do a lot of rewriting, crossing out, and scribbling. Any operation can be done more efficiently using digital devices. We live in the 21st century, and even though I see the appeal of writing on paper (see Chapter 1), I still believe that humans should use the contemporary tools available to them. I will show you a great alternative to the traditional notepad, but remember, it's you who's doing the testing here. You're the one who should decide which tool suits you the best and is the most efficient for you.

The progress of technology and apps like Nozbe allow us to easily create projects; change their names; and easily move tasks, notes, and files between them. All it takes is a few clicks of a mouse or touches on a screen. This kind of flexibility is incredibly important; while doing tasks, many projects end up changing or joining together, and the tasks get moved around or disappear. It's all easier done with a digital tool.

## Project layout in Nozbe

In Nozbe, after going into the Projects tab you will see a list of your active projects. Here you can add new ones, naming them based on the tips given earlier. After selecting a specific project, you can see which tasks it contains. If it's a new project, the list of tasks will be empty; it's just waiting for you to fill it up with your actions.

The list of projects in Nozbe is flat. This means that you can't add sub-projects or sub-subprojects. It's a simple hierarchy; there are projects, and in those projects are tasks. Why did we choose such a structure? You will soon find out.

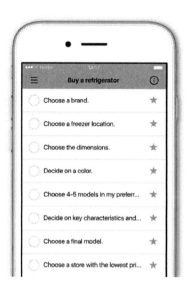

## Move tasks to their projects

When reviewing your inbox view, you can easily drag any task and drop it into its desired project. You could also simply click on the task and in its details change the parameter from inbox to a project from your list.

If the task can't be assigned to any of your existing projects and it's not a two-minute action that you can complete right away, you may want to create an additional project called "miscellaneous," and put it there. Many people have such a project for loose ends.

As we've already learned, it's best to name tasks some-thing short using a verb. Nevertheless, sometimes a task requires a longer description or additional information that will help you get it done quicker in the future. In Nozbe, you can use the comments feature in such cases. Go into the task's details and add a text comment, image, or a short checklist. If the task is to call someone, just put the phone number and other useful information into this comment. If you have errands to run, add the opening hours and the address of the specific store as a comment.

## When to use checklists instead of projects?

At the beginning of the chapter, I quoted David Allen who believes that any action that requires multiple steps is a project. Although this is true in most cases, there are some exceptions.

I've learned from experience that sometimes in order to optimally list activities, I need something between a project and a task—a task with a list of small steps. In Nozbe, all you need to do is add a comment to a task in the form of a checklist and outline what needs to be done step by step.

**This is especially useful when:**

- a task requires a bit of time but not more than a few hours,
- a task is made up of a few steps that I simply don't want to forget.

Going back to the examples from the beginning of the chapter, "New Post on Blog" can be a project if it really is a complex blog post. It could also be a task requiring a few steps: planning it out, writing it, finding a suitable image, posting, and promoting it on social media. Everything depends on the level of complexity of what we want to achieve and the amount of time it will take. I'd leave "Buying a Fridge" in the form of a project, because it requires many steps that aren't directly connected and would probably be done over the course of a few days.

**Other examples with checklists:**
- A list of ingredients required to make a dish (the project is the entire recipe and the task is "Prepare the necessary ingredients")
- List of things to pack for a weekend trip (the project is, for example, "Memorial Day Picnic" and the task is "Pack the backpack")
- Fruits and vegetables to buy (the project is "Shopping" and the task is "Shop at the grocery store")

Thanks to this kind of approach, you will have a clear list of projects and a few tasks in each of them; those tasks that require a few small steps will have checklists attached to them.

## Do all projects need to be completed?

The definition of a project that I've adopted is a bit more flexible than the one described by Allen. On my list in Nozbe, you'll find two types of projects:

- **Goal-oriented projects** – These have a concrete goal and once they are achieved, the project is finished. An example of such a project would be "Buying a Fridge"—once you've bought it, the project is closed.
- **Ongoing projects** – These, on the other hand, are never finished because they are a list of tasks or activities concerning a specific aspect of my professional or personal life. For instance, I have a project entitled "Marketing" in which I put all loose tasks that have to do with marketing. I also have a project called "Personal Affairs" that I fill with all the tasks to be done after work that aren't connected to any goal-oriented project.

Projects are simply lists of tasks, and it's up to you to decide which are going to be goal-oriented and which are going to be ongoing. On my list, you can find several of both types.

## How to make some projects stand out from the list

In Nozbe, there's an option to assign a color to a project. By default, all projects are light gray, but if you assign a color to them, they quickly stand out on the list. Some people even use the colors to assign a status to a project, similar to a traffic light: green is "go," yellow is "problems," and red is "critical." With project colors, you have flexibility to design your project list the way you want.

## Too many projects? Use labels!

The flat list of projects in Nozbe is easy to master, but the more obligations pile up, the harder it is to find specific projects and group the similar ones that you want to work on right now.

This is when labels intended to group similar projects come in handy. When you want to focus only on specific projects and hide the rest, all you need to do is assign those projects a common label, and choose it from the project list to see them.

## Here are a few examples:

- Create a label entitled "Blog," and label all projects related to running your blog (posts, updates, social media, etc.).
- Create a label entitled "Company," and mark all company projects.
- You can also have an "Inactive" label where you put projects that have started but are on hold for an unspecified time, e.g. the client is not yet sure whether to move forward, but you already have some useful information for the project (as suggested by Kristóf from the book's launch team).

- You can even create a label entitled "Get to work!" and label all the projects that you want to get done by the end of the week

There are many possibilities. I myself have over 100 projects in Nozbe and fewer than 10 labels to help me manage them.

## What if the same goal-oriented project needs to be repeated often or regularly?

Everyone's job, from time to time, involves the repetition of some activities. In situations like this, digital tools come in especially handy—thanks to technology, you don't need to keep on writing the same things over and over again.

In Nozbe, you can tackle recurring activities using project templates. If a goal-oriented project is a collection of tasks that you have to fulfill every so often, save it as a template. After that, all it takes is a few simple actions to create that project again and begin getting things done.

If you're a freelancer, you probably have a steady list of tasks having to do with starting a job for a new client. So, creating a template entitled "New Client" to include them all can be useful. You'll save yourself some valuable time and will optimize the process of accepting new business. If you clean your house every year during the spring, create a template entitled "Spring Cleaning" and include all the odd corners of the house you must check.

If you must travel for work often, create a template entitled "Things to Pack," and from now on you'll never forget anything.

Since it's helpful to make use of other people's experiences, I encourage you to take a look at the templates created by other Nozbe users at the Nozbe.how page. There you'll find, amongst other things, my list of tasks necessary for a successful start in a triathlon, a set of exercises to prepare for a 10-kilometer run, recipes for delicious dishes, and travel tips. As you've probably noticed, the bonuses at the end of each chapter of this book are also published in the form of templates that you could import into your Nozbe account.

# **Exercise:** Change one major task into a project

The name of the task that has become a project:

Steps (tasks) required to get this project done:

- [ ]
- [ ]
- [ ]
- [ ]
- [ ]
- [ ]

## Exercise: Change one major task into a project.

Choose one task from your inbox that requires a few steps and divide it into smaller tasks. Name them by describing the specific physical activity that you have to do using verbs. To make things easier, imagine yourself doing the activities. This will help you create a specific task and use the right verb to motivate yourself to work. Congratulations, this is your first project!

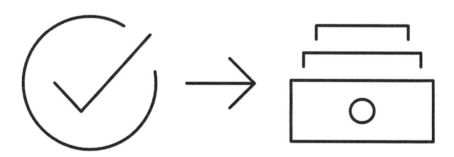

## Chapter 2 Action Plan: Sort your tasks into projects

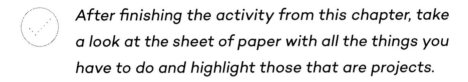

*After finishing the activity from this chapter, take a look at the sheet of paper with all the things you have to do and highlight those that are projects.*

*Convert the tasks into projects, making sure that they include as many small tasks as you are able to come up with.*

*Look through your list, paying attention to the task names. Are all of them clear and motivating? If not, change them using the tips in this chapter.*

**Good luck!**

**Bonus materials:** If you want to find out more about managing projects and completing them efficiently, download this package of practical articles, templates, and videos I've prepared for you on the topic.
**ProductivityCourses.com/bonus**

In this chapter, you will learn

# how to find the next actionable step to move a project forward, and how to prioritize your tasks in order to have a productive day.

# **Step 3.** Focus on What's Most Important

---

*How to find and prioritize actions that will help move your projects forward*

Once you've sorted your inbox into tasks and projects, it's time to get some of them accomplished.

Do you often ask yourself, "What should I do next?" Well, in this chapter, I'll help you figure out two very important aspects of productivity: how to find the next physical action to move a project forward, and how to prioritize your task list in order to have a very productive day.

If you were able to finish the activities from the two previous chapters, you most likely have a long list of projects with many tasks assigned to each. Where should you start? How do you get all of this in order? What should you focus on? Crying is not an option...

## How to approach a project

Let me give you a hint: Each time you tackle a new project, take a look at its list of tasks and consider which could be the next action. Which of these tasks will get you moving as quickly as possible towards your goal at this moment?

Why is this so important? We can't look at a list of tasks the same way we do a self-regulating system. We must always start with the first task in order to get to the second, and so on. Since exceptions prove the rule, you must know that sometimes it's the first task that blocks the progress of your project. Very often the next action to take is not that obvious... but once you've found the right one, everything starts moving forward!

The key to success is the theory of small victories. According to this theory, as long as you accomplish even the smallest task in a project—whatever it may be—you will immediately see measurable results from your work, feel better about yourself, and gain momentum and motivation to keep the project going. This is how you get things done!

## Sample project: Baking a Cake

We can't bake a cake until someone goes grocery shopping, we can't go grocery shopping before we choose a recipe, and we can't choose a recipe until we find out what kind of a cake the rest of the family wants. This is a classic case of a cascade of tasks coming one after another. However, not all of them are connected! We can, for example, wash the cake pans that will have to be washed at some point. This way we take the first step, which, although doesn't get us very close to a fully baked and iced cake, it can help us get started. So, it turns out that washing the pans can be the starting point of the project "Baking a Cake."

If you limit the time you take to make a decision, you can move more quickly toward your goal. Even deciding on the type of cake can be tricky. Part of your family is going to want a cheesecake, and the rest may want a chocolate cake! In this kind of a situation, it's best to take a vote (apply the Two-Minute Rule) and then smoothly move on to choosing a recipe.

The next action is going to be shopping, which we could always delegate to someone else in the house (more about this in Chapter 5). The project has taken off, and before you know it, you'll be enjoying a delicious cake.

## Prioritizing your next actions—how to get them all done?

Now that you've found your next actions in your projects, it's time to prioritize them. Not all next actions are created equal, and not all projects have to be moved forward right this minute. Each day, it's up to you to decide which tasks to do first and which can be left for later. The next part of this chapter will hopefully help you with these decisions.

## Start off with the big rocks—the most important tasks for today

To illustrate the problem of choosing the order of your tasks to work on, let me tell you a story about "big rocks," which I've found very helpful:

*A certain professor showed his students a large, empty jar during a lecture. Next to it he had a stack of rocks—some large, others small, and*

*some smaller still. He also brought out a bit of sand. The professor proceeded to put the largest rocks into the jar. After that, he added the slightly smaller ones, then the even smaller ones, and lastly, he poured the sand, which filled the empty spaces in the jar completely. After he was done, he asked the students, "Why did I put the rocks into the jar in this order?" Someone in the room responded, "Because if you had first filled the jar with the sand and small rocks, there wouldn't be enough room for the large ones, sir!"*

The same goes for tasks. If instead of focusing on the key tasks, you decide to start with the most trivial ones, you may come to realize that the day has ended, and you no longer have the time to do that thing that was really the most important.

This is why it's important to always set one, two, or three goals for the day. In the book *The One Thing*, Gary Keller and Jay Papasan argue that it's best to limit oneself to the bare minimum. They suggest deciding on one key goal for the day and treating all other matters as secondary. Kristóf, a member of this book's launch team, suggested going 1-3-5, meaning finding your one thing for the day, your three other big tasks, and five smaller tasks that ideally should also be done on the same day.

I do something in between. Before going to sleep, I write up to three things that I'd like to get done the next day. According to many theories and studies, during sleep the human mind subconsciously begins working on what we plan to do after waking up. In the morning, I again read these three tasks, save them at the top of my list of priorities, and begin the work day starting with them. I try to avoid social media and email until I finish at least one of these three key tasks. Later, I continue with other next actions from other projects on my list.

## Priorities in practice using Nozbe

I'd like to again show you how easy it is to manage your priorities and get them done using a digital system like Nozbe.

As you already know from the previous chapter, you can create many projects and put many tasks in each of them in the app. Once you've figured out which task from the given project is your next action, you can mark it with a star; this way, it will appear on your Priority task list in Nozbe. Any starred task automatically appears on this list. The order of tasks on the Priority list is independent from the order in their corresponding projects.

Furthermore, to help you make sure the Priority list is complete and truly your command center, some tasks in Nozbe will be assigned a star automatically. Let's take a look at when that happens.

## When tasks automatically become priorities

Let's suppose that in one of the projects, you've got a task with a completion date set to "today." The system will automatically highlight it with a star, and it will appear on the list of priorities without you having to do anything. Thanks to this, no important meeting or date will slip past you.

I used to occasionally forget about some of my obligations. Today, I know that if I set an exact date for a task in Nozbe, even if it completely slips my mind, the system will mark it as a priority and send me a notification on the day that it's due.

Sometimes I know that I won't be able to deal with a task set to be completed today, but I'll happily work on it the next day. So I postpone the task by assigning it the status "tomorrow" and retract its star. I know that the Nozbe system will mark the task with a star tomorrow and move it back onto my list of priorities. If you're sharing a project with a team (which we'll talk more about in Chapter 5), and someone delegates a task to you, it will automatically be marked with a star by the system as well. So you don't need to worry about missing something. If your list of priorities for a day is too long, you can filter it using parameters such as deadline, duration of a task, as well as other criteria (more about this in Chapter 6). This helps narrow down the list of tasks and lets you concentrate on those you can see on the list. With this condensed view, you will witness your productivity skyrocket!

**A tip: Focus on what's most important**

*Remember not to mark all tasks as priorities. This would only undermine the purpose. Also, you can have entire projects without any pressing next action. It all depends how you'd like to set it up.*

# **Exercise:** Your priorities

Choose three priorities out of the tasks you listed in Chapter 1.

## Chapter 3 Action Plan: Choose your priorities

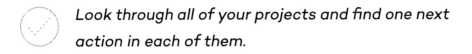 *Look through all of your projects and find one next action in each of them.*

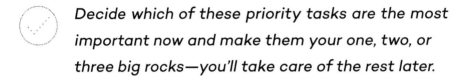 *Decide which of these priority tasks are the most important now and make them your one, two, or three big rocks—you'll take care of the rest later.*

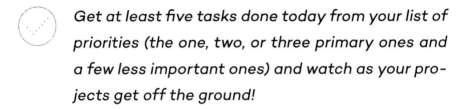 *Get at least five tasks done today from your list of priorities (the one, two, or three primary ones and a few less important ones) and watch as your projects get off the ground!*

**Good luck!**

 **Bonus materials:** If you'd like to learn more about deciding on next actions, you can download a package of practical articles, templates, and videos that I've prepared for you.
**ProductivityCourse.com/bonus**

In this chapter, you will learn

# that thanks to amazing technology, we can be truly productive anywhere, anytime.

# **Step 4.** Be Productive Anytime and Anywhere

*How to work efficiently using modern mobile devices and the cloud*

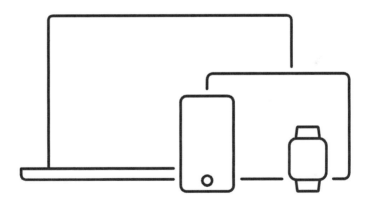

The beauty of the 21st century is that thanks to amazing technology, we can be truly productive anywhere, anytime. In my company, we even take it to a different level as we work in a "no office" system. This means each of us works at home, and we don't have a central office. Thanks to the power of the internet, we are able to communicate and work efficiently. This way of operating our business has compelled us to form certain habits and master tools that allow us to perform tasks from any place on earth, using any device we choose: computer, tablet, smartphone... you name it!

If you work in a more traditional setting and you commute to an office, you can still benefit from choosing tools that come in handy with remote jobs. This way, even when you're not at the office, you'll have access to your data and work system, and you'll always be able to work efficiently and get things done wherever you are!

## Paper doesn't synchronize with anything!

Some books on productivity and time management encourage their readers to use sheets of paper, post-it notes, or paper calendars. I even mentioned this method as an option in the earlier chapters of this book. Exercises on paper can help with understanding certain matters, but I wouldn't encourage you to build a system based on pen and paper alone.

Nowadays, access to the internet is nearly limitless. We have advanced 4G (LTE) mobile networks and extensive fiber-optic connections. We've got ever-improving portable computers, tablets, and smartphones. I think that individuals should make use of the solutions that technology offers and build their productivity systems based on them.

Sheets of paper don't synchronize with anything, and it's hard to reorganize things on a sheet of paper. Moreover, if you write something important on paper and leave it at home, you won't have any way of getting ahold of that information! When someone in your household accidentally throws a piece of paper out with the garbage, your notes will be gone forever. One way is to use a smartphone camera to take a picture of your physical notes, but there are even better ways!

## Internet cloud

Have you heard of internet cloud storage? Productive people aren't afraid of it. In case you don't know what I'm talking about, let me explain: When you save data in the cloud, it's safely stored on remote servers, and all you need to access it is a device that can connect to the internet like a computer, smartphone, or tablet.

This is the way electronic mail has worked for years. Messages can be saved on your local disk, but far more importantly, they are saved on the operator's server. Your list of contacts works the same way when you synchronize it with Apple, Google, or Microsoft systems. You can extend this logic to how you treat most of your data. I'll show you how I make use of the cloud's potential using a modern smartphone.

## Access to everything using my iPhone

Technology has come so far that I can access all of the data that I might need to do my job from my smartphone.

iPhones automatically connect you to Apple's cloud called iCloud. Thanks to this, all of my contacts, emails, and other data saved on my phone are also stored on the cloud—on Apple's servers. Each night as I charge my phone, backups of my smartphone's information are automatically updated on Apple's servers. Thanks to this, even if my iPhone is stolen, broken, or lost, all I have to do is buy another one and log in to iCloud. By doing so, all of my previous phone's contents will be downloaded from the cloud, and I will regain access to all of my data as if nothing had ever happened.

Furthermore, most of my smartphone's applications save data on the cloud. For example, I can access:

- Emails (on iCloud as well as Google)
- Presentations and documents created with Apple's Keynote, Numbers, or Pages software (on iCloud)
- Microsoft Office documents (on OneDrive)
- Documents created together with other coworkers (on Google Drive)
- Any other documents (on Dropbox servers)
- Notes (on Evernote's servers)
- Tasks and projects (synchronized with Nozbe servers)
- Pictures (on iCloud Photos, although some pictures are stored on Google Photos or Flickr)

It's options like these that ensure that I've got access to all the resources necessary for work on my phone. My tablet and laptop work the same way. All of my data from these three devices are always synchronized, and I can be productive and switch devices whenever I need. This is how one should work in the 21st century! I'm a fan of Apple, so I use an iPhone. However, smartphones from other brands, especially with the Android operating system, can be similarly configured.

## The cloud and data security

There are many perks to storing data in the cloud. The most important one is that it guarantees access to your data from anywhere (so long as there's an internet connection) using the device of your choice.

Businesses that store their clients' data in the cloud take many precautions to make sure their infrastructure protects these resources. Despite this, many people do not trust this method of data storage. The idea of sending key documents and information to someone's outside servers makes them nervous. However, when your computer stops working or your phone falls into a lake, your files are safe—as long as they are stored in the cloud.

Some companies that use the cloud have thousands and sometimes even millions of users, so they know how to create and maintain the infrastructure of backups as well as encrypt the information they store. They must ensure that their clients' data are safe at all times—it's their bread and butter. Otherwise, they would go out of business. Of course, it doesn't hurt to follow the basic rules of data security:

- Use longer passwords that are composed of multiple words or random symbols.
- Use a password manager such as 1Password or KeePass so that you don't save passwords in text documents or (oh, the humanity) on a piece of paper lying next to the computer.
- Whenever possible, use a multi-factor authentication option, so that in addition to entering your username and password, you are required to verify the login with a code sent via text message.

## Mobile applications

Another advantage of keeping data stored in the cloud is that you can access it via mobile applications that are optimized for your device. I'm a big fan of working on tablets. I even wrote a book entitled *#iPadOnly*. In it, I show that there are many practical applications for tablets that enable you to work efficiently and comfortably. Heck, I'm even editing this chapter on my iPad Pro right now.

Anyway, these applications have been optimized for smaller screens and touch performance, which makes working on a tablet comfortable and many times even easier than working on a traditional computer.

The same goes for applications on smartphones. Not only are they simple and easy to use, but they also make use of the extra features, such as the phone's camera or GPS system. Want to attach a picture to a comment on a task? Snap and it's ready! Looking for the closest dentist office? GPS satellites together with Google Maps will help you find the right one!

Many applications are also designed to work even when the internet connection is flaky. After reconnecting to the internet, all data is synchronized with the cloud. This feature is one of Nozbe's key advantages.

## Practical uses of the cloud

Using and storing data on the cloud considerably simplifies working on multiple devices and with coworkers. The following examples illustrate some common situation.

### Example 1: Shopping

*When I'm out shopping, I use a shopping list saved in Nozbe. I check off each product I buy in the project that I share with my wife. Whenever my wife (whether she's at home or at work) remembers anything else we might need, she adds it to our mutual project. The information automatically ends up in my pocket... in the Nozbe application on my iPhone, and my wife is happy that I didn't forget to get anything. If my wife had given me a piece of paper with a list of everything we need before I went out, she wouldn't have any means of adding more items to it. I wouldn't have been able to buy everything that she had wanted.*

### Example 2: Note

*I drove the kids to school and on the way back, I was already at work in my thoughts. I came up with a great idea, and I saved it in my phone's notepad. After returning to the office, I sat at the computer and opened an application for taking notes. My notes were already there, waiting for me, and I was able to immediately pick up where I left off and get to work. I didn't even have to reach for my phone anymore.*

**Example 3: Waiting room**

*I'm waiting for my appointment at the dentist's office. I'm very nervous, and in the waiting room, there's only a stack of magazines describing lives of celebrities who really don't interest me. So, in order to have something to do, I whip out my smartphone and finish working on a blog post, which I had already started writing at the office. This allows me to work and focus on something important, rather than waste time reading pointless magazines and getting irritated in the process.*

**Example 4: Preparations**

*(from Claire, a launch team member and Nozbe user) I prepare for meetings at my laptop by making notes in Evernote, then I take my iPad to meetings and reference the notes I made and take additional notes. I can easily review my notes later from my laptop or even my phone in a pinch!*

## The existence of the cloud makes founding more "no office" types of companies possible

As I mentioned at the beginning of this chapter, I don't believe that technology's latest achievements should be reserved for only unconventional companies such as mine (we don't have a central office, despite growing our team to more than 25 people).

Perhaps it would make sense to use the potential of modern technology and allow some of your workers to work remotely, if not full time then maybe at least a few days a week. Wouldn't it be nice to travel and, thanks to the ability to work remotely, not have to give up your current job? Don't tell me that you've never had to deal with work-related matters when you're away from the office... This is why keeping data on the cloud is so important!

# **Exercise:** Your cloud-based tools

Think of the programs you use to save data on the cloud. Make a list of the ones you know and the ones you are planning to check out.

1. 
2. 
3. 
4. 
5. 
6. 
7. 
8. 

1. 
2. 
3. 
4. 
5. 
6. 
7. 
8.

## Chapter 4 Action Plan: Embrace the cloud, and work from wherever you want!

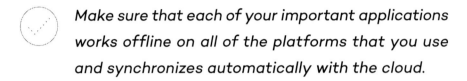 *Make sure that each of your important applications works offline on all of the platforms that you use and synchronizes automatically with the cloud.*

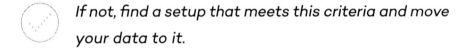 *If not, find a setup that meets this criteria and move your data to it.*

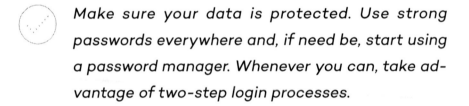 *Make sure your data is protected. Use strong passwords everywhere and, if need be, start using a password manager. Whenever you can, take advantage of two-step login processes.*

**Good luck!**

 **Bonus materials:** If you'd like to get even more tips on how to work efficiently no matter the time or place, you can download a package of practical articles, templates, and videos on the perks of modern technology, the internet cloud, and mobile applications!
**ProductivityCourse.com/bonus**

In this chapter, you will learn

how to efficiently collaborate with others and delegate tasks because even if you have managed to perfect the previous steps in this book, the day still lasts only 24 hours.

# **Step 5.** Delegate Tasks to Achieve More—Work as a Team

*How to efficiently collaborate with people and communicate through tasks*

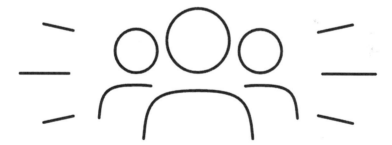

Successful teams utilize skills and foster open communication, but for optimal collaboration, teams must also master task distribution. In this chapter, you will learn how to increase productivity by delegating and communicating through tasks.

We'll start off with some examples of cooperation among roommates and finish with building an effective company team. Paradoxically, the tips in this chapter will come in handy even for people who consider themselves "lone wolves." I'll demonstrate that even if you've managed to perfect the previous steps in this book (arranging projects, setting priorities, and discovering possibilities of working anywhere), the day still lasts only 24 hours. If you want to achieve success and stretch your day beyond that, you have to learn how to work with others.

## What would I do differently if I were starting today?

This is one of the most-asked questions I hear from those attending my lectures and conference presentations: **"If you could go back in time and create Nozbe again, what would you do differently?"**

Many would have answered a question like this by saying they wouldn't change a thing, that each lesson was equally important. Though I generally agree with this, there is one thing that I would change: I'd hire my employees much sooner. For the first year, I worked practically alone. The second year, I hired the first programmer, and the third year a person for customer support. It was only during the fourth year that I started building a real team. Now I know that I should have gone about it completely differently. I'm not talking about creating jobs, but rather finding help from specialists in a variety of fields sooner.

## Are you a hardhead who wants to do it all yourself?

Everyone has heard lines such as these many times: "You're saying that I can't do it?", "You think I can't handle it?", "You want something done, you do it yourself." I get the impression that this kind of attitude has been hardwired into people's minds. We often insist on doing things on our own and fear trusting others. We think that we know everything or simply don't want to hand over control. I felt the same when I was entering the world of business.

## We aren't the best at everything!

During the first couple of years of working at Nozbe, I handled everything: writing the code, developing new app functions, creating marketing materials, answering emails, promoting products, contacting the press, managing invoices, etc. It goes without saying: I had to start somewhere, but am I an expert in all of these fields? Of course not. The revelation that I can't handle everything on my own hit me late in the process. That's why I am writing this—so that you don't repeat my mistakes.

## The more the merrier... and the faster!

Let's begin with a simple example sent in by Andrew from the publishing team:

**How do I take care of spring cleaning at home over one weekend?"**

**There are two options:**

1. *You can send the members of your household on a walk to the park and do the cleaning yourself (obviously, "I know how to do it best") or...*

2. *Sit down with everyone Saturday morning to figure out what needs to be cleaned and what everyone does best. Split up the tasks and get to work.*

*Which of these options seems to be more practical, quicker, and perhaps, most importantly, more realistic to accomplish within the timeframe? I believe it's the second one.*

*But beware! For there is no rose without a thorn! Especially when working with the younger members of your household, you'll likely have to explain something several times and sometimes fix their mistakes or point things out. However, once they know what they are doing, the cleaning will prove to be a fun project, and its effects may exceed your expectations!*

## There are 24 hours in a day!

Sadly, a day is always 24 hours long for each and every one of us. It's impossible to stretch or bend time (if you somehow figure out how to do it, please do let me know!). The only way of extending a day that I know of is asking for help from others. Just look at those who achieved success:

- **Kevin Durant**, one of the best basketball players of all time, is surrounded by advisors, managers, physiotherapists as well as many others who help him achieve success both on and off the court.
- **Warren Buffett**, the fourth wealthiest person in the world, and considered by some to be one of the most successful investors in the world, doesn't manage all his businesses and investments alone; he's surrounded by trusted people.
- **Elon Musk**, the creator of Tesla electric cars and SpaceX rockets, wouldn't be able to manage without a team of excellent scientists and entrepreneurs.
- **Michael Hyatt**, a super-popular author, blogger, and speaker works with an entire network of team members and freelancers who help him deliver valuable products and content.

In order to achieve success, it's worth accepting that others can be equally capable or even better at accomplishing a task as you are. Be open to working with others—share tasks and realize goals together as a team.

## Superheroes don't exist!

The people mentioned above realize that they aren't experts at everything! They hire people who are better than they are in the fields that they need help with.

Kevin Durant is a competitive basketball player, but he's also a great investor. Why? Because he has advisors who help him with investment decisions. Michael Hyatt is knowledgeable about the art of publishing, creating a platform, and building an audience, but he still makes use of those who are better at audio and video editing.

Once I woke up and finally hired my first programmer, I made sure to choose someone who was much better at it than I was. I wanted to be sure that he'd be able to make significant improvements to my app. Today, the development team of Nozbe is composed solely of geniuses. In the art of programing, I can't hold a candle to them, and that's exactly how it should be! It's thanks to their great knowledge and experience that our product is evolving quicker and better than ever before.

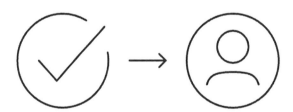

## Begin slowly and learn how to delegate tasks

As I've already mentioned in the above example of spring cleaning, learning how to let go of absolute control should start at home. How? By dividing responsibilities, clearly defining the tasks, and jointly deciding on the goals. And I don't mean "passing the buck," but rather accomplishing goals together and complementing each other's work.

## "I'll do it faster on my own!"

If you think that explaining things to others is a waste of time, please think again. I'm sure you're thinking that it would be quicker to tackle things solo rather than to explain it to someone, and then be stuck fixing their mistakes afterward, right? I felt the same way when I was starting up my business.

Try to look at things this way: It's an investment! Once a coworker understands your expectations, he or she will surely be able to do a stellar job. Allow yourself to be surprised and feel relieved. Should things not work out ideally at first, talk it over. You'll make some changes, and next time around things can only get better!

This is why I stressed at the beginning of this chapter that I should have hired more people sooner—not necessarily immediately full time, but to do specific tasks, such as corrections on the webpage. This is something that would take a graphic designer up to an hour to do, but would eat up two full days of work for me. I also could have asked a programmer friend of mine to add a function that took me a whole week to implement—something he would have been able to do not only much faster, but probably better.

I was afraid that hiring other people to do things would consume too much time, energy, and money. It didn't occur to me back then that I could have started off by either offering friendly barter, a favor for a favor, or hiring a freelancer who would work on an hourly basis. This way,

I could have saved myself a lot of time that could have been spent doing other tasks.

Even now, when we have over 25 people working full time, we also work with 10 translators (our application is available in 10 different languages). They aren't hired employees, but they still regularly receive texts from us to translate, and at the end of each month, they issue an invoice based on the number of translated words. Nozbe is only one of their clients, but since we work with them regularly they know that they can often count on receiving translation commissions from us. We, on the other hand, know that we can count on them when we need their services. This kind of a system is beneficial for both sides.

## The first steps toward teamwork

Since you already know that I'm not trying to convince you to hire a swarm of workers—that I'm simply encouraging you to make a habit of hiring people to do some tasks—it's time to move on to the practical side of things. How should you delegate tasks effectively? How do we work together?

Let's say you're writing a blog that's starting to gain popularity. You want to get your friend who's a graphic designer to update your website's look. How do you do this? You can make use of the popular S.M.A.R.T. system for designating tasks (its mnemonic name stands for "Specific, Measurable, Actionable, Realistic, Time-bound"):

- **S – Specific** – Convey to the designer exactly what you expect. In this case: fix the colors of the blog, change the page's layout, redesign the logo, and make use of some photos from the last photo session.

- **M – Measurable** – Decide together with the designer what should be focused on first and foremost, how many different versions you would need in order to accept it, and how you are going to measure the progress of the project.

- **A – Actionable** – Figure out together what steps need to be taken to get it done, what makes sense as well as what would require too much work or money and can be put off to a later date.

- **R – Realistic** – In order to ensure that the designer does a stellar job, it's worth getting them motivated and eager to work, but set realistic expectations.

- **T – Time-bound** – Decide when the work must be finished. It's crucial to have a specific date in mind so that the job doesn't go on forever. When do you want the projects ready? When do you need the final versions? When does the new page need to be up and running? When do you want it officially published?

As you can see, in order for such a project to be successful you need to clarify many different details as early as the planning stage. It's good to keep in contact with the contractor to ensure the correct and timely completion of the job.

## Let's start the collaboration!

I'm sure you're asking yourself right now, how do I collaborate with a designer? Well, it all starts with your commitment. Keeping track of as much information about the project as possible is one of your responsibilities. It's worth using the S.M.A.R.T. criteria as a guideline for describing all the different aspects of your project. The more you jot down, the better. This way, the designer knows exactly what to expect and will have all the guidelines written down in one place, like in an email or some other kind of message from you.

## Now let's get down to talking about business

I recommend making direct contact via telephone or meeting the contractor only after writing out and sending all of the specifications of the job. This way both sides have time to prepare for the conversation after they've acquainted themselves with the specifics of the job. Many people begin talks before they've drawn up the details, making meetings unproductive and the process take much longer than it has to. To improve efficiency, adopt this principle: First I write, then I talk... and then I write once again.

If you don't know what exactly you need, you aren't going to be able to properly give instructions to the other person. If you don't first write down what you want to talk about, you can't expect your partner to understand or remember everything that they need to know. This is why it's so important to have a conversation based on a list of guidelines; it allows you to take notes, explain unclear elements, and add new ideas and findings on the fly.

## After the conversation, send them your notes

Furthermore, after a meeting like this, it's worth sending the other party a summary to make sure that both sides understand the issues discussed.

## Monitor the project's progress

Afterward, you'll need to stay up-to-date and monitor the project, for example, via email. All new information must be put into writing and sent to the contractor, and any questions must be answered without undue delay.

## When everyone's doing what they're supposed to be doing, your blog flourishes.

Thanks to this kind of help, you are able to focus on preparing valuable content for the blog and promoting it, while your designer takes care of the look of the page. All you have to do is stay in touch and keep an eye on the project, rather than learn how to design a website from scratch. This way, you will definitely achieve your goal much quicker and the effect will be better than if you had done it on your own. Your blog readers will appreciate this!

## Asynchronous cooperation is the key to success

In the above example, I am proposing asynchronous cooperation, meaning the kind where "in order to work efficiently together, we work separately." In the case of synchronous cooperation, we constantly trade information and expect immediate reactions from each other, often bothering and interrupting each other's focus. In the case of asynchronous work, we respect the modus operandi of our partner.

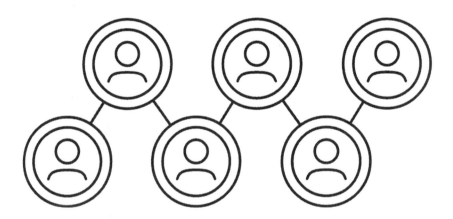

When working asynchronously, you first have to prepare the job order for the designer on your own. This can take quite a bit of time, because it requires you to thoroughly establish your S.M.A.R.T. objectives, draw out preliminary specifications, and list any ideas you might have. Now you can get your partner involved; you talk about the specifications of the job and again make a note of what you decide on. Then each of you can begin working on your respective tasks, every now and then checking up on the other's progress.

Thanks to this way of doing things, no one gets in anyone's way. Everyone's got time to concentrate on the project and familiarize themselves with it. When something needs to be discussed, the conversation is based on the information prepared in advance rather than on abstract ideas. These days, people often take the completely opposite approach. They say:

- Let's meet up and discuss the topic.
- I'll swing by your place, and we'll talk.
- Let's arrange a meeting, and we'll discuss everything then.

This kind of thinking leads to long and ineffective meetings that merely create the need for more of them... and they don't require anyone to properly prepare themselves beforehand. I'll repeat the mantra: First I write, then I talk... and then I'll write once again.

## Email is a good starting point but...

In the above example, I suggested that email is a good means of communication between two people working together. I think that it's a helpful tool when you are learning how to work with others.

However, today, it's easy to notice a glaring flaw of email inboxes: there are simply too many messages. We receive tens, if not hundreds, of them daily. Because of this, key messages get lost among all the newsletters and spam. To make things worse, when working on a project with many people at the same time, a lot of information is lost in the flood of emails, and it gets increasingly hard to keep up-to-date on the project.

This is why I'm an advocate of separating communication with close associates from the rest of the world. Furthermore, since we're working on common projects, it's more efficient to communicate through tasks rather than email messages. Sending each other emails compels us on a subconscious level to talk, whereas using tasks forces us to work. Which, by the way, is what this is all about! That's why in my company we haven't sent each other emails in years. Instead, we communicate by using tasks in Nozbe.

## Communicating through tasks in a system for managing projects

Just as in previous chapters, in order to illustrate the most interesting elements on the subject, I'll describe the practical aspects of teamwork using Nozbe as an example. Nozbe has many competitors on the market, such as Asana, Basecamp, Wrike, and Trello. Choosing one is a matter of individual taste, which I'll leave to you. For obvious reasons, I feel the most comfortable working in Nozbe, especially since the application was designed to meet the criteria described in this chapter.

## Working with a designer using Nozbe

Let's return to the example of contracting a designer to improve the look of my blog. If both sides are using Nozbe, all you need to do is create a new project using a title such as "Redesigning the Blog" and invite the designer to it. Next, add the tasks connected with the project, for example:

- Develop specifications for the redesign.
- Prepare an initial estimate.
- Discuss the specification, and agree upon expectations.

Now, all that's left to do is to delegate the work to the appropriate person, meaning that in the case of each task you'll need to assign the person who will be responsible for it. After you've done this, the chosen person will be notified. This way, the designer will definitely see the tasks and know to start working on them.

Furthermore, a comment can be added to each task in order to iron out the details. Comments can consist of regular text, checklist, graphics, pictures, and even PDF or Word documents. They can also be attachments from external services such as Dropbox, Google Drive, and Evernote. Whenever a comment appears in a task (for example, containing a question from a contractor or early suggestions and sketches), you'll also see it in the dedicated view in Nozbe.

## Transparency of information in shared projects

When sharing a project in Nozbe, everyone involved can see what stage each task is at, read attached comments, or add new ones for clarification. This way, it's easier to manage all the elements of the project and keep track of each other's work in order to successfully complete it.

Whenever you want to add more people to the project, all you've got to do is invite them via their email address. As soon as their invitations are accepted, new associates gain access to all the data contained within the project without having to send them any messages, files, or any other sort of information.

## My wife and household matters...

As we end this chapter, I'd like to share another real-life example.

My wife wasn't happy with me taking too long to answer her emails, especially since a few of them demanded rather immediate action. I told her that I've been very busy lately with work and receive a multitude of messages every day from all sorts of different people, so the ones from her tended to get lost in the flood of correspondence. To avoid this, I came up with the following solution: I created a project in Nozbe entitled "Household Matters" and invited my wife to it. She then exported the previously sent emails into our shared project. She did it by sending all of her messages to her dedicated Nozbe email address, specifying in the messages' subjects which project they should end up in and who (me!) should be assigned to them. The emails were automatically converted into tasks and assigned to me. Thanks to all of that, they ended up on my list of priorities.

So my wife's requests suddenly appeared in my priorities for the day. I got to work on them, and whenever I'd have doubts, I'd add comments asking her to be more specific and delegated the task back to her. After writing the necessary pointers, she would again re-assign the task to me, and by the end of the day, all the tasks were *done. My solution allowed us to both focus on doing the tasks rather than on corresponding. From that day on, we started dealing with most matters using shared projects.*

## Don't work on your own—you'll achieve more!

I hope that this chapter has motivated you to try working with others. It is the only way to achieve true success! Start slowly with small tasks and projects, and you'll soon realize that building a real team is within your grasp!

Remember the title of that song by Michael Jackson, "You Are Not Alone," because indeed, you really are not alone. If you want to achieve success, you shouldn't act like you are!

# Exercise:
# Who could
# help you out?

Make a list of people with whom you can cooperate.
Think of who could help you get your projects done.
Who is a specialist in a field you know very little about?

| Task | Person |
| --- | --- |
| | |
| | |
| | |
| | |
| | |
| | |
| | |

## Chapter 5 Action Plan: Involve others

✓ *Think of a project you're working on that could use some outside help, and choose a task that someone else can take care of.*

✓ *Consider how to convince that person to work with you and help you out.*

✓ *If you use Nozbe, try out the project-sharing function instead of sending email messages when working together.*

✓ *Assign tasks and work in a team to achieve more!*

**Good luck!**

**Bonus materials:** If you want to gain access to even more valuable information on how to effectively communicate and cooperate, download today this pack of practical articles, templates, and videos on working in a team! **ProductivityCourse.com/bonus**

In this chapter, you will learn

# how to freely connect tasks from different projects. You'll discover their similarities and consequently organize your work in a way that will make you even more efficient.

# **Step 6.** Group Your Tasks and Shift Gears!

---

*How batching tasks in categories (or contexts) will skyrocket your productivity*

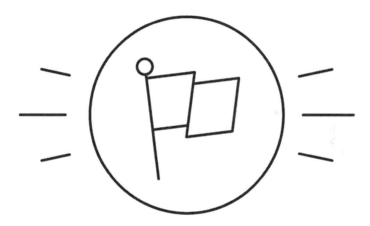

To take your productivity to new levels, you need to keep simplifying and optimizing all actions. In this chapter, you will learn how to quickly and efficiently get similar tasks done using categories, even if they're from different projects. It's like a whole second dimension of task management, and it works brilliantly. Please bear in mind that my concept of categories in this chapter is very similar to how David Allen defines "contexts" in his book, *Getting Things Done*.

At this point, you've already mastered the art of adding tasks, putting them in projects, and getting your priorities done. If you're also working with others, there's no doubt in my mind that you'll be successful!

This chapter will help you achieve an even higher level of productivity. You'll be able to freely connect tasks from different projects. You'll discover their similarities and consequently organize your work in a way that will make you even more efficient.

## Before I tell you what categories are, here's a quick example:

*It's a regular work day. It's approaching 3 p.m. I've just eaten a delicious lunch. I'm full and have returned to my desk, but I really don't feel like working. As a matter of fact, I feel like taking a nap, but due to all of my responsibilities I can't allow myself to take one. What can I do to return to my regular work rhythm?*

*Usually in situations like this, I take care of matters that don't require too much work yet bring quick results, like making some calls. First, I call my wife in order to find out what she's up to—and even though our conversation is usually short, we really enjoy it. Next, I look in my projects for tasks that I can take care of with a quick phone call, and I start making these calls. After each call, I can see that the work is moving forward, and again I begin to feel very productive. I manage to take care of things, despite feeling sluggish after eating!*

This example shows how easy it was for me to regain my vigor. All I did was find the tasks in my projects that had one thing in common—they required a phone call—in other words, they involved the use of a specific tool. Identifying these tasks took me only a second, because I had already marked each of them as requiring a phone call. This way, all I had to do was filter them by this category, and I was able to take care of a few things that weren't even on my list of priorities!

## What are categories?

Although you're working on tasks from different projects, you often do them using similar tools or working in comparable conditions. This is where categories come into play. Here are a few examples:

## Tools:

- "Smartphone" – you use your phone in order to take care of a few unrelated matters from different projects
- "Computer" – it's sometimes easier to do certain things on computers than on mobile devices
- "Printer" – certain documents from multiple projects require printing

But don't stop there, here's an example from Kristóf, our publishing team member and a Nozbe user:

> **Example**: "I have a category called 'Bank.' This means the online banking platform (which is a type of a tool) of my bank. By using this category, I can arrange transfers (both work and personal) and other bank-related tasks (checking the credit card statement, etc.) in one sitting. Thus, I do not need to log in and out of the online banking system multiple times."

## Places:

- "At the Office" - things that need to be done when at work
- "At Home" - things that can be taken care of only at home
- "Away from home" or "Errands"- in order to not forget to go to the post office, do the shopping, buy flowers, etc.

Again, Kristóf has a great example:

> **Example**: *"Our office has a document storage outside of the office. I have a category named 'storage.' Whenever I need something from that storage (or when I need to take something there), I mark it with this category. This way the task is in its dedicated project, but I can use the category to see the whole list when I am in our storage. Quite useful."*

## Ways of handling the task, time, and other variables:

- "Whenever" – tasks that aren't among the most important, but it would be nice to take care of them whenever you find the time
- "Writing" – for tasks that require drafting longer texts
- "Frog" – when a task is particularly important and is one of the key tasks for this day. (This reference comes from Brian Tracy's book, *Eat That Frog!*.)
- "Waiting For" – when a task is waiting for the other party to respond; very useful when working with clients

Csaba from our book launch team has a very good example of this:

> **Example:** *"I have a category called 'blocked,' and I marked it with a red exclamation mark in Nozbe. Whenever I have a task which requires further action that cannot be done right now or when a task assumes the completion of another task, I mark it with the 'blocked' category. I also put a short message in the comment section to remind myself what prevents me from completing that task. This is a handy function when I work with a lot of interdependent tasks."*

Categories can help group similar tasks from different projects together so they can be batched and done all at once, thus saving time.

Thanks to grouping tasks by category, you are able to quickly perform similar actions at once and move on to other matters that require other tools or situations.

## Places as a category or as a separate project?

Christopher, a Nozbe user from our launch team, pointed out the need to explain the difference between the category "At Home" and the project "Household Matters." How can these similarly named categories and projects not conflict with each other? Here are some examples that will show you the difference between categories and projects:

> *Example: The task "Schedule a Doctor's Appointment" can be in the "Household Matters" project, but we can also assign it the category "At the Office" because registration at the clinic is only available until 4 p.m., so you'd have to call while at the office. Likewise, you may find the task "Prepare Documents for the Boss" in the "Work Matters" project, but if those documents are at home, you'll assign it the "At Home" category.*

## Even a person can be a category

In the previous chapter, we discussed the rules of working together on projects. Let's see how categories can further improve your teamwork.

My wife created a category entitled "Boss." Whenever she has a task that she needs to discuss with her superior, she assigns it this category, no matter what project it is associated with. When she prepares for a meeting with her boss, she prints all of the tasks marked with this category and can be sure not to forget to mention anything important.

## Activities can also be categories

According to my schedule, the day that I devote to writing is Thursday. That's when I check which tasks are assigned the "Writing" category. These may involve all sorts of different projects: my blog posts, articles for the Nozbe blog, columns published in other media, sales and marketing material, etc. So when Thursday comes around, with this category I'm able to easily group the tasks that require a writer's touch, filter out the rest, and get to work.

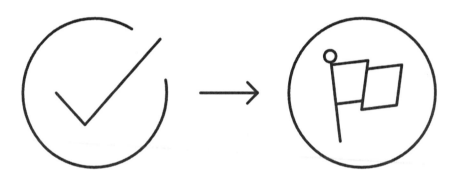

## Categorize—it's worth it!

Categories are like having an extra weapon in your arsenal, because they allow you to group tasks from different projects depending on where and with what tools they are meant to be accomplished.

How you want to treat and assign categories is completely up to you—you'll want to figure out how they can be of use to you and then put them into practice. Just as in the case of everything else, it's best not to overdo it. Too many categories can end up making life even more complicated and impede the efficiency of your productivity system.

## Categorizing tasks in Nozbe

Digital tools for managing tasks are equipped with simple functions that allow the categorization of tasks. In Nozbe, for instance, all you need to do is assign your tasks the appropriate categories. Then, you can go to the Categories tab and choose whichever one you intend to work on. You can also filter your list of priorities using the categories you had assigned to the tasks.

For example, today I'm working on writing this chapter, and I've got over 50 tasks on my list of priorities in Nozbe. In order to focus on writing and editing texts, I used a filter in order to isolate the tasks on my priority list marked with the category "Writing." Now I'm only faced with five tasks.

Some people really have a whole system for categories in Nozbe, just like Claire from our publishing team:

*"I group my categories by a prefix character. I put a comma in front of a location (,Anywhere*

*,Computer ,Office ,Phone); a dot in front of a priority (.A-High Priority .B-Medium Priority .C-Low Priority/Someday .D-Delegate); and a colon in front of timeframe that it's due (:Due - November :Due - December). This helps me know that I should only choose one with each prefix, and it also automatically sorts the categories how I want to see them. I also chose icons to go with each category just for fun!"*

## You can also create an "Urgent!" category

My assistant designates tasks to me in Nozbe quite often, but in order to differentiate the ones that she thinks require my more immediate attention she additionally categorizes them as "Urgent!" This allows me to see immediately which matters are truly pressing, and it's these tasks that I focus on first when starting to work.

This kind of category could, of course, be useful in other cases, not only when working with an assistant. It can prove useful when your list of priorities is becoming dangerously long and it's hard to identify key tasks. Just assign your goals for the day the "Urgent!" category, and you will be able to single them out and get to work on them as soon as possible.

In Nozbe, a single task can be marked with multiple categories, which gives the user even more flexibility. When assigning the task "Call the Editor Of XYZ Magazine" to me, my assistant can also mark it with both the "Phone" and "Urgent!" categories. This way, it doesn't matter whether I intend to make some phone calls or focus on the most important matters—it won't escape my attention!

## You don't need to categorize every task

Michelle from our book launch team suggested highlighting this; you really don't have to categorize everything, but you really should use this feature to your advantage when needed. She says:

*"I don't use categories in Nozbe on a regular basis, and very often try out a new category scheme and abandon it just as quickly. However, when my priority or another list gets too long, I find it helpful to apply some context to the list of tasks, which can be done quickly using the multiple edit tool. Then filtering by category helps me feel more in control of a long list. I may not end up using those categories again and usually don't take the time to add a category when I am creating tasks. But it's a nice feature to be able to take a few minutes to categorize on the fly when I need it to batch tasks together."*

# Exercise:
# Your categories

What task categories do you apply in your everyday work? What other tags could help you group your tasks in order to get things done efficiently?

| Task | Category |
|------|----------|
|      |          |
|      |          |
|      |          |
|      |          |

## Chapter 6 Action Plan: Group tasks

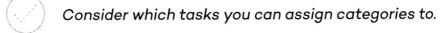 *Create a basic list of categories. You can use examples from this chapter.*

*Consider which tasks you can assign categories to.*

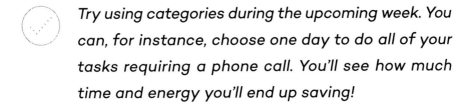 *Try using categories during the upcoming week. You can, for instance, choose one day to do all of your tasks requiring a phone call. You'll see how much time and energy you'll end up saving!*

**Good luck!**

 **Bonus materials:** If you want to learn more about the art of grouping similar tasks, download here a package of practical articles, templates, and videos on the perks of using categories! **ProductivityCourse.com/bonus**

In this chapter, you will learn

# how to take care of your reference materials and organize your documents so they are always available, helping you efficiently complete your tasks.

# **Step 7.** Take Control of Your Documents

---

*How to deal with reference materials that will help you get stuff done*

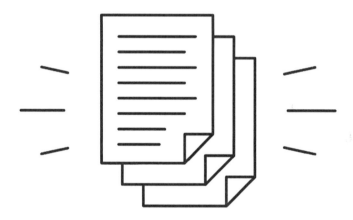

Invoices, email attachments, PDF files, letters, contracts, etc. pop up in my inbox every single day. I bet that the same goes for you. Some of these documents may be important while doing certain tasks, but some of them can also turn out to be an additional burden you may have to simply deal with. In this chapter, I'll explain how I take care of my reference materials and give you examples of how you can organize your documents so they are always available, helping you efficiently complete your tasks.

## Think "paperless"—digitize your paper documents so you can access them anywhere

Although the law has yet to catch up with the digitalization of our world and often requires us to keep invoices, bills, contracts, and other documents in physical form, I still recommend digitizing, meaning creating digital copies, of all the important documents you receive. Be careful not to just scan/digitize everything, though, because that can create digital clutter. There are some things we can simply throw away or shred without scanning. If you save them to the cloud (see Chapter 4), you'll have access to them no matter the time or place!

## My home office system: my drawer, scanner (phone), and paper shredder

Let's start off with my home office's spacious drawer for documents that I keep thematically sorted in folders:

- House – notarial deeds, contracts with media providers, etc.
- Vehicles – proofs of purchase, registration, insurance, etc.
- Family – birth certificates, passports, etc.
- Achievements – diplomas, souvenirs from competitions, etc.
- Bills – bills of sale and warranties for more expensive items from the last two years, etc.

- Invoices – company invoices, which I later hand over to the accountant

I have each of these paper documents also digitized and saved in the cloud. This way I have access to a digital copy of each and every important document in my drawer from any device I have at hand.

One of our book launch team members and a Nozbe user Kristóf shares his story to confirm the practicality of digitizing everything:

*"I have all my family's important documents (IDs, tax cards, health insurance cards, etc.) scanned and stored in Evernote. This way, whenever I need to fill in an application or data sheet (about any family member), I have the information on my phone. It is also useful to scan and save to the cloud insurance certificates and vouchers when travelling.*

*I also scan every contract, declaration, court decision, and other important documents at work (we are a law firm). Almost every week, a client or a former client will ask for a copy of a document that was issued years ago. By having the documents scanned and stored on our server, I do not need to dig it up from the document storage. This saves a lot of time and headaches."*

**Here is how a document ends up in my inbox:**

## Example 1: Credit card from the bank

1. I received a letter from the bank with a new credit card enclosed.
2. The letter ends up in my inbox (see Chapter 1).
3. I open the envelope and see the new credit card, so I immediately log into my bank account and activate the card (Two-Minute Rule).
4. Next, I look through the document that came with it and check if it contains any important information that's worth saving or storing. If there's nothing worth keeping, I toss the document into the shredder (it does contain my personal information).
5. I put away the card, and throw out the envelope. All done.
6. Additional (optional) step: I put the card information details into a safe password-keeper app, like 1Password or Keepass. This way, I have access to all the card's details without having it in my wallet. Keeping card info in digital form makes it easy to fill out the forms when paying for shopping online.

## Example 2: Bill of sale for furniture

1. I bought a sofa for the living room and put the bill of sale into my physical inbox.
2. Looking through the inbox, I take out the bill and scan it with my phone.

3. After scanning the bill, I save it on the computer (or in a cloud service like Evernote) and put the original in my "Bill" folder in my home office. This way, I have a physical copy of it in case of a refund or warranty repair.

> **Important:** I don't do this with all of my bills and receipts. I only do this with the ones that are for more expensive products. In the case of receipts for less expensive products, I simply scan them and toss them into the paper shredder, hoping that a digital version of them will do (although I'm aware that in certain stores and countries it may not be sufficient). In the case of receipts for products below a certain price range (let's say, $10 or $20), I simply shred them immediately because I usually wouldn't ask for a refund for such items.

## Example 3: Correspondence requesting payment for electricity, media, land, taxes, etc.

1. I've received an electric bill. As usual, documents like this end up in my inbox.
2. When looking through the inbox, I take the document and scan it with my phone.
3. If the law requires me to keep such a document, I put it into an appropriate folder, otherwise it disappears in the shredder.

4. If I'm making a payment like this for the first time (for example, after changing a provider, moving, or buying a new service), I create a recurring payment at the bank, or add a recurring task in Nozbe and attach a digital version of the document as a comment to that task.

## Why should you read all your letters only once?

As a last example, I'd like to recall a part of one of David Allen's seminars:

> I had received a letter. I picked it up and read it. It contained some information that was very important, so I created a corresponding task in my system. After that, I tore up the letter and threw it into the garbage. Done.
>
> The person standing next to me then asked, "But David, that was a letter! How could you simply destroy it just like that?!" Then I thought, "Certainly, it was a letter, but I'm not going to be reading it a second time or framing it. The letter contained information, I reacted to it... and now I no longer need it!"

It was after this seminar that I decided that I'll no longer hoard documents but instead begin to effectively manage them and make quick decisions on what to do with each letter and bill.

## How do I create digital copies of documents? Where should I keep them?

There are a few ways of scanning and storing documents. We will start with the simplest and finish with the most advanced way.

## Method 1: Scanner at the office and files on a computer

This is the most traditional approach. We've got a scanner in my office that's plugged into a computer. We put a document into it, scan it, and save it in digital format on the disk.

I recommend keeping documents in folders with simple hierarchies, for example, a folder entitled "Documents," a subfolder entitled "2016," and use detailed file names such as "Bill-ikea-couch.pdf." All modern computers are equipped with very good search functions, so finding a bill for a couch from IKEA will be very quick and simple.

## Method 2: Scanner on a phone and files in the cloud

Most of us actually already have a "scanner" of sorts— our smartphones. There are many great applications for taking photos of documents. They recognize paper and use filters that make the photographed document look as if it were scanned. Additionally, many of them also use OCR, which is a technology that recognizes text in a document and makes it "searchable."

These applications synchronize with the cloud, and photos scanned like this can be immediately saved in iCloud, Dropbox, Google Drive, Box, OneDrive, etc. This significantly simplifies the process of digitizing documents: whip out your smartphone, take a photo of your document, assign the photo an appropriate title, and save it in the cloud. The computers at home or at work automatically synchronize with the cloud, and as a result, the file is available not only on your phone but also on your computer and on any other device.

> **Practical tip:** *Jolanda, our publishing team member and a Nozbe user, explains: "When I buy something that comes with a paper manual, I try to find that manual online (from the manufacturer's website or elsewhere), download it, and throw out the paper version. I'm saving a lot of space like this, and making it easier to find exactly what I am looking for by searching for a keyword in the manual."*

## Method 3: The Evernote application on a smartphone

You can cut corners even more and try out my favorite method using the Evernote application. All I need to do is turn it on and take a photo of a document on my phone. Evernote will turn the photograph into a scanned document and save it in the cloud in the form of a note, which after a quick synchronization, is viewable on all of my devices. Another plus is that thanks to the OCR function, Evernote is able to recognize the text in an image file, which makes searching for files easier.

As you already know, I strongly recommend storing files in the cloud (see Chapter 4) because this makes all of your documents accessible on all of your devices, wherever you may be! While some documents can simply be kept (for example, bills or photos) in an appropriate directory on a hard drive, others are necessary for completing certain tasks. The key to maximum productivity is storing documents of the second kind as auxiliary materials in their respective projects and tasks in order to always have them on-hand.

I'll demonstrate how I do it in Nozbe. You'll see how easy it is to attach documents directly to projects or tasks.

## Reference materials in Nozbe

When you're working on complex tasks, having reference materials like documents, images, or photos easily available will save you time. Reference materials are not always necessary, but when a task requires a document, you don't want the frustration of stopping and searching for it. You need a modern productivity application, such as Nozbe, that allows you to attach documentation to your tasks, giving you direct access to all the relevant information.

Nozbe users can add comments to their tasks in the form of regular text, text files, images, PDFs, short checklists, YouTube videos, or even links to websites. If you use cloud services like Evernote, Dropbox, or Google Drive, you can very easily attach files from them directly to your tasks in Nozbe.

One of our publishing team members, Csaba, finds advantages to using both Nozbe and Evernote:

*"Whenever I find a new job advertisement, or receive a call for a proposal with a well-defined deadline and long description, I save it to Evernote, add a reminder, and then it appears in Nozbe as a single task. I give it a due date in Nozbe, so I will be reminded when the deadline is approaching and I can see all the details as an Evernote attachment. Now I can work on this task with high confidence."*

## Encrypting documents in Nozbe

Nozbe is used not only by individual clients from all over the world, but also by teams (see Chapter 5), including governments, offices, law firms, and public administration institutions, which is why we decided to fully encrypt documents that are attached to tasks and projects. This way, when you create a task in Nozbe and add a comment in the form of a file, it will be encrypted and uploaded onto our servers, thus being protected from unauthorized individuals. It will be available only to you and the people with whom you've shared the project that contains the task.

## Working with versions of documents in Nozbe

If you're sharing a project with someone and delegate them a task with an attached document, they can download and work on it. Then, all they need to do is save the document and upload the new version to the same task in Nozbe, and in the history of the task's comments you'll be able to view all versions of the document with the dates they were added. This makes following the progress of your project easier and also lets you avoid exchanging emails, changing the titles of any subsequent versions of the same file, and any similar procedures. You keep the full history of actions and, at the same time, still have access to the newest version of the document.

## It's time to figure out your own way of managing reference materials

Very often to get a task done, you'll find that you still need more information for its execution. A properly created system for storing reference materials can significantly improve your work, especially when working on the most complex tasks. It's worth dedicating some time to properly organize such a system so that you can make good use of it later. When you know where your documents are both in physical and digital forms, you'll never waste unnecessary time searching for them!

*Extra tip: As Sanjay from our publishing team puts it, "One of the areas where I use Nozbe for key documents is the dates of yearly/five-yearly/ten-yearly renewals for visas, passports, licenses, and memberships of professional organizations. Linking the dates of renewal to the digital archive of these certificates or documents ensures that I'm never in the situation of being in an airport with an expired passport or driver's license."*

# **Exercise:** Managing your documents

1. How do you manage your documents now? Where do you store your documents and reference materials?

2. How could you improve the process of saving and storing your documents? What tools and apps would you want to use?

## Chapter 7 Action Plan: Sort out your archive!

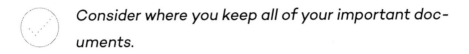 Consider where you keep all of your important documents.

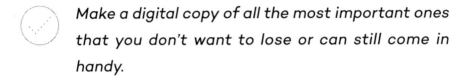 Make a digital copy of all the most important ones that you don't want to lose or can still come in handy.

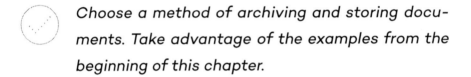 Choose a method of archiving and storing documents. Take advantage of the examples from the beginning of this chapter.

**Good luck!**

 **Bonus materials:** If you want to expand your knowledge on how to manage documents, use the bonus materials I've prepared for you. Download today your package of practical articles, templates, and videos!
**ProductivityCourse.com/bonus**

In this chapter, you will learn

# how to set aside an hour or two each week for some time with yourself, during which you'll check and update your productivity system.

# **Step 8.** Check Your System Regularly

*How to arrange a meeting with yourself once a week to keep yourself up-to-date*

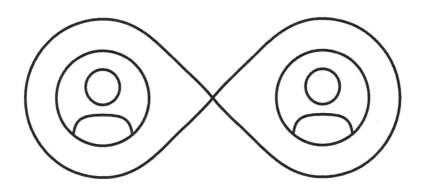

After reading the previous chapters, you already know how to clear your mind, organize your tasks into projects, set priorities, work from anywhere, collaborate with others, and make use of categories and reference materials. You've got this!

Nevertheless, if you don't perform regular reviews of your system, things may end up spiraling out of control. In this chapter, I'll teach you how to set aside an hour or two each week for some time with yourself, during which you'll check and update your productivity system. This weekly review is potentially one of the most important meetings you'll ever have... each week!

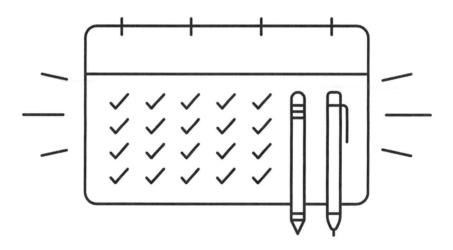

## Why are "weekly reviews" so important?

Productivity experts suggest arranging systematic, weekly meetings with yourself in order to go through what you've already done and what you want to accomplish in the near future. David Allen in *Getting Things Done* calls such a summary a "weekly review." He says it's a time when you plan activities for the upcoming week.

Allen believes that this is the only time he ever actually thinks about what he has to do, and afterward, he simply does it all since he knows that he'll have time to think about things again next week.

**For me, weekly reviews are extremely important for a few reasons.**

- I get a chance to calmly **summarize the week** and figure out what I managed (or didn't manage) to accomplish.
- Going through my **calendar**, I see what awaits me the following week, and I'm able to properly prepare for it.
- While **reviewing all of my projects**, I have a chance to motivate myself to work harder on what I've already started or decide to withdraw from certain commitments.
- I can simply take the time to think about **where I'm headed** and whether it's in the right direction.

Weekly meetings with oneself is a key element of every productivity system. Thanks to them, you're able to really make sure you're getting the right things done.

## Regularity is the key to success!

It's hard to be methodical. It seems we're always too busy to be able to properly divide our time among many different things and people. Finding two hours for a review often proves to be quite a challenge. While we tend to have no problem finding time to meet with others, we tend to fall short when arranging meetings with ourselves.

I've also noticed that for many people, such one- or two-hour sessions may seem like a boring and fruitless exercise. It's easy to get the impression that it's a waste of time, since instead of simply "doing," you're forcing yourself to review what there is to do, right?

## Are you living your life?

You've got a choice: you can either "go with the flow" of life and let others decide where you go, or you can take matters into your own hands. If you don't regularly review your system, tasks, projects, and goals, you'll quickly start drifting aimlessly, reacting only to what others have planned for you. The weekly review brings context to your tasks and projects. You need time to determine whether your actions are on course with your desired outcomes.

## How often should you schedule a "weekly review"?

Though ideally reviews should be done weekly, there is a minimum. At the Getting Things Done (GTD) Summit conference in 2009 that I attended, it was said "a weekly review must be done at least once a month." It sounds silly but it's true: a month is the maximum amount of time that you will be able to keep a proper course without verifying and sorting all the aspects of your activities. Based on my experience and that of thousands of Nozbe users, after more than a month without a proper review, you stop feeling that you're in charge of your life.

This is why you must try to never delay your weekly reviews for more than a month. One-on-one meetings with your productivity system are meant to be moments of reflection. During a week, many things can go wrong, which is why a review is your chance for a quick course correction and an additional opportunity to make more conscious decisions for the next week.

As my mom would say, "Thanks to your review, you'll approach your next week with more understanding."

## How to determine a good time and date for the weekly review

Everyone approaches these meetings differently. Some people have them on Fridays, some on Mondays, some over the weekend. As I've already mentioned, your review doesn't need to last half a day! Sometimes, it only takes an hour or two to get everything sorted out, especially if you review regularly.

I once confided in my friend with whom I co-wrote the book *#iPadOnly* that I have a hard time getting into my weekly reviews. I asked for advice and got the following response:

*"For me, weekly reviews are a full ritual. First of all, I don't do it at home, I instead drive over to the nearest Starbucks. Once there, I find a comfortable spot in a leather chair. Next, I order*

> *a specially-made coffee that I never drink on any other occasion. I sit in the chair with the coffee and my iPad, put on a pair of headphones, turn on my 'weekly review music,' Beethoven's 9th Symphony, and begin the review!"*

This example really appealed to me, so I decided to take a few pointers from it and created a similar ritual for myself. Come Friday morning, I drive my daughter to school and rather than go back to my office, I go to my favorite café for a coffee and a glass of freshly squeezed orange juice. I sit in the corner, put on my noise-cancelling headphones, turn on Ludovico Einaudi's concert at The Royal Albert Hall, and begin the review. I don't leave the café until I've finished.

Not everyone can leave their office to do a weekly review, so it's important to also be able to do it there. Many people "hack" their company's systems to be able to set aside a two-hour window to themselves. Some simply put an official meeting in the company calendar to let others know they are "in a meeting." I even heard that some book a conference room for this occasion to assure no one "accidentally" walks into their office.

## Monday or Friday... or the weekend?

Some people prefer to do the weekly review on the weekends, others choose Friday, some Monday and there are even folks who do their review in the middle of their work week. You'll have to find the time that fits best into your schedule, but to make it easier for you, let me offer a few helpful tips.

Regarding days of the week, I used to do my review on Mondays but recently I switched to Fridays. I realized that planning my week in advance is just better. As we discussed in Chapter 3 about "priorities," it's really helpful to plan your day ahead by determining your most important tasks the evening before. Turns out the same logic applies to the weekly review. Doing my review on Fridays gives me a peace of mind for the weekend and a fool-proof Action Plan for Monday.

Even though it used to work for me, I now try not to do my review on a weekend. For many people weekends are ideal, but once my circumstances changed, it no longer fit my lifestyle. I like to spend my weekends with my family without interruptions, so Fridays works for me, but your situation may vary.

You might also want to go the extra mile and constitute an official "company policy" for everyone to do a weekly review on Fridays. I've done that in my company and we actually completely redesigned Fridays in our team—everyone is required to do a "weekly review" as their most important task for Friday. The rest of the day can be designed however they want though we encourage them to focus on personal development and learning new skills. We call this policy "TGIF," Thank Goodness It's Friday. If you want to learn more about it, you'll find the link to the articles I've written about in the bonus materials for this chapter.

## My weekly review step-by-step

I've added a project template of my weekly review to the bonus content for this chapter, so make sure to download it after you've finished reading. Feel free to use my template as a blueprint and tweak it to your liking to create a successful weekly review. Below is the gist of my process:

## Preparation

Before beginning the review, I make sure that I've cleared out all of my inboxes (see Chapter 1). I especially make sure to clear and scan the papers from my physical inbox at my home office so that I have access to all of it. After that, I'm ready to start.

## A quiet moment

I first try to find some peace (I'm Catholic, so I pray for five minutes, giving thanks to God for the great life He's blessed me with). After that, I turn on the music and get to work!

## Clearing out inboxes and writing down ideas

I've already cleared out the inbox in my office, so now it's time to clear my inbox view in Nozbe. In it, I often find ideas, notes, and information from which I create new tasks, and sometimes even new projects. I check my emails and look at other materials that I hadn't had the chance to review earlier. If something comes to mind that I haven't yet written down this week, I do it immediately and assign it to the appropriate project.

## Calendar

I go through my last week's meetings and do the final review of the meeting notes to make sure no actionable item escapes my attention. I review what I have planned for the upcoming week and make sure that all the scheduled commitments are still taking place and I'm ready for them.

## Weekly summary

I check the statistics of all of my and the company's webpages and any other data that I should be monitoring. I open a special spreadsheet in which I input some of the information and compare it to the previous week's, looking at the trends. I either have a reason to be proud or to be worried. Reviewing these statistics gives me some guidance as to where to focus my work in the upcoming week.

## Checking goals

Aside from specific projects and tasks, I also review personal goals, both long- and short-term. Setting goals helps me direct my attention and commitments. They remind me of my values and where I'm actually headed.

Thanks to them, I'm able to plan out my actions and create additional projects if needed.

People approach goals differently and keep track of them in various ways. I keep them in Nozbe in separate "special" projects. I create a different project for each area of my life and start each project's name with "Goals -," like this: "Goals - family," "Goals - company," "Goals - fitness," etc. Each goal within each area is a separate task. While doing my weekly review, I review each goal and see how close I've gotten to it, what's still missing, what requires more work, and what I should be focusing more on. I use the comments section of each task or goal to update it with additional thoughts or ideas. The conclusions I draw from this part of the review often end up becoming an inspiration for new tasks or projects in my productivity system.

One of our Nozbe users Kristóf gives a different example of keeping track of goals:

*"I create a note in Evernote for each weekly review with the date as the title. The note includes my goals for the year, my goals for the quarter, my goals for the month, and the goals for the current week. I duplicate this note when I start the weekly review and go through the yearly, quarterly, monthly goals as a reminder, and review what was accomplished from the weekly*

*goals. I do not delete the long-term goals after completing them, but make them bold instead. This way I can see what was done and be happy about it. I set my weekly goals at the end of the weekly review. Each quarter, I have a 'deeper' review and determine the goals for the next quarter."*

## Reviewing projects

I review all of my projects in Nozbe. I click each of them one by one and check the tasks in them, sometimes changing the deadlines, adding comments, removing tasks, modifying them, and exporting them to other projects or to my Priority list. I also often create new tasks for me and my coworkers.

Reviewing all of my projects tends to take some time, but it's the only way that I can be sure that all of my data is up-to-date and in-line with my goals.

It's important to check each project and decide whether it needs a well-defined next action. Sometimes during a hectic week, we forget to define the next step in a project after completing a task. The weekly review is the perfect opportunity to add a next action in all those projects where there should be one, or schedule the most important tasks that require deep work or more research.

### Reviewing priorities

Next, I check my list of priorities and organize them. I move, change, and arrange them. I even try to do some tasks immediately according to the Two-Minute Rule mentioned in the foreword of this book.

### Finishing up

Once I've gone through all of the above stages, I again pray and thank God for the great week I've had and ask Him for the wisdom that I'll need to get through the next one. I sometimes like to listen to an upbeat song in celebration of a successful weekly review.

### That's all!

Maintaining a systemized and regular approach is key here. Try to do regular reviews every week. This is your regularly scheduled meeting with yourself—one of the most important meetings you'll have during the entire week. This meeting not only ensures that you stay on top of things but also that you have a peace of mind over the weekend to spend quality time with your family or friends, knowing that you've reviewed your week and you've got the next one planned.

# **Exercise:** Your weekly review

When will you do your weekly review (day of the week)?

_____

What time will you begin?

_____

Where will you work on it?

_____

Why did you choose this particular time and place?

_____

_____

_____

_____

_____

_____

## Chapter 8 Action Plan: Schedule your first review!

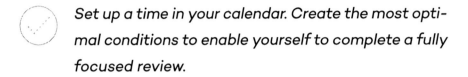 *Set up a time in your calendar. Create the most optimal conditions to enable yourself to complete a fully focused review.*

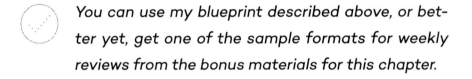 *You can use my blueprint described above, or better yet, get one of the sample formats for weekly reviews from the bonus materials for this chapter.*

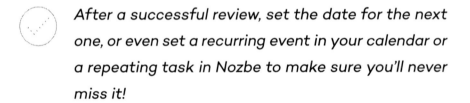 *After a successful review, set the date for the next one, or even set a recurring event in your calendar or a repeating task in Nozbe to make sure you'll never miss it!*

**Good luck!**

 **Bonus materials:** If you want to learn more about how to regularly check the performance of your productivity system, download now this package of practical articles, templates, and videos that I've prepared for you. **ProductivityCourse.com/bonus**

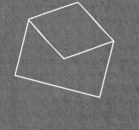

In this chapter, you will learn

# how to deal with the constant flood of messages that you receive every day and integrate email into your productivity system.

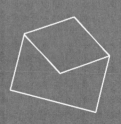

# Step 9.
## Master Your Emails

*How to zero your inbox and deal with email overflow*

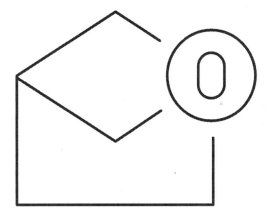

After tasks, projects, and a good review, I'd like to close this book with a few additional tips and tricks that you can put to good use starting now. In this chapter, you will learn my best email practices, and find out how to deal with the constant flood of messages that you receive every day. I'll show you how to integrate email into your productivity system. Your tool for managing tasks will play an incredibly important role here. It could be Nozbe or any other system that's equipped with most of the functions described in the previous chapters.

## More action, less management!

Remember, the goal of systems for managing time, tasks, and projects is not the actual management and constant sorting of tasks but really getting to the "done" state! Carl from our publishing team wrote something very interesting on this topic:

> "When I first started using Nozbe, it was just a great tool for sorting and managing my affairs. I spent a whole lot of time tagging, moving, writing tasks, and so on. However, at some point I realized I was going about things the wrong way. Suddenly, Nozbe became the place where I gathered all of my tasks for their realization. I write and describe them as much as is necessary and when I'm ready, I get them done! At this point, Nozbe has become a practical tool to work with, just like a telephone, computer, email, or even a car."

Why am I mentioning this in a chapter dedicated to emails? Because I've noticed that many people have a very similar attitude towards email. They check them every moment they can, read them several times, move them to all sorts of different folders, sort them, assign priorities... and then are surprised that they can't handle such a big pile of messages!

## Forget "checking" email!

I'd like to stress that I no longer "check" my emails. I simply "process" them. Perhaps this sounds a little odd, but the difference is substantial. When you take care of something, it is finished, but when you only check something, it still requires acting and finalizing. Many people check their emails constantly and read the same messages multiple times. This isn't very effective. The ultimate goal of yours should be to "touch" each email once, and only once. Sounds easier said than done, but the tips below should help.

## Zeroing your inbox

I believe that the habit of zeroing your inbox, the act of completely clearing it out, is one of the pillars of productivity. When I log into my email, I always decide what to do with each message that I've received—whether it is a task that needs to be done, something I need to respond to now or later, or something that I should archive or delete immediately if it's completely useless to me.

## The Two-Minute Rule

When answering emails, I often use the previously mentioned Two-Minute Rule (see Foreword). If answering the message will take less than two minutes, I do it immediately. Because I use my iPhone and iPad very often, I've learned to quickly send brief and concise responses. Now that dictation on mobile devices have started working more reliably, I use it to quickly dictate an answer and be done with it.

People prefer to receive short messages as opposed to no message at all. These days, you don't have to treat emails like traditional letters. Every recipient cares only about the concrete information, so skip the noise and cut to the chase!

The aforementioned co-author of the book *#iPadOnly*, Augusto Pinaud, afraid that some people may still take offense to short responses, always adds a signature to the end of his emails: Sent from my iPhone, even if he wrote the message on a computer.

Of course, I'm not encouraging any kind of deception, but I still think this is a clever way of reminding both yourself and the recipient that these days, it's the speed of the response that matters (see Chapter 4).

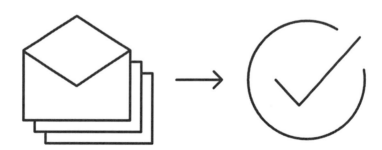

## Sending emails to a program

Some applications feature the option of creating an individual email address that allows you to send data to it. I make use of this feature in Evernote and Nozbe every day. I send tasks and articles to myself, which are immediately added to the system. In order to speed up the whole process, I've added my Nozbe and Evernote addresses to my list of contacts. These "email gateways" have proven to be very useful. When an email's contents are suitable for conversion to a task, I forward them to Nozbe. Behind the scenes, the title of the message becomes the name of the task, and its contents a comment. Sweet!

In the bonus material attached to this chapter, you'll find exact instructions for this function as well as tricks that will enable you to get even more use out of it (like a cheat-sheet of using #hashtags to move the task to the right project or category).

If the email contains some vital information like an invoice, bill, or confirmation from an airline, I send it to Evernote. Despite the fact that email inboxes these days offer quite a large amount of storage space, I prefer to conscientiously export important data to a place where I keep most of my documents. Thanks to this option of transferring emails to apps directly from my inbox, I don't have to leave my emails, and I can process them faster.

## Newsletters and other automatically sent messages

Shopping as well as registering for services online involves handing over an email address, usually resulting in an inbox full of unwanted messages. There are a few ways of dealing with this.

**Separate filter** – If you use Gmail and your address is namesurname@gmail.com, you can register to outside services as: namesurname+newsletter@gmail.com. When you do this, emails that arrive will be automatically assigned the tag "Newsletter."

**Separate email address** – When registering to services, use a different email address from the one that you use for private and business correspondences. This way, commercial messages won't get mixed up with the truly important ones that require a response.

Gmail also introduced the **Social and Promotion tabs**, which automatically filter these kinds of messages. It's definitely a good thing, but I still think it's best to take matters into your own hands to be sure that we get the fewest unwanted messages as possible.

It's also worth going through your commercial messages once a week after your weekly review (see Chapter 8), because some of them can contain important information or discounts for products that might interest you. It might be worth simply **unsubscribing from other newsletters**.

All it takes is clicking the right link at the end of a message (unsubscribe, manage notifications, etc.).

Some people use additional services that manage and unsubscribe you from newsletters. You'll find links to these services in bonus materials at the end of this chapter. It's also useful to add filters in Gmail to label things you want "to read" and even have separate inboxes for each label ("waiting for," "to read," "to do"). Like that, you can keep your inbox empty.

## Notifications from services, especially social media

Social media sites send tons of notifications. You should log in to every site that you use and turn off all unwanted notifications. Often these settings are hard to find, but spending a few minutes configuring them will save you a lot of time in the long run. For instance, you can do this on Facebook by clicking Menu, and then choosing in sequence: Settings / Notification / Email.

## Filters, folders, and organizing your email's inbox

Aside from the active struggle with spam, commercial messages, and notifications, we don't need many filters. People used to have the habit of creating separate folders and filters for every person in order to sort their correspondence. But as I said at the beginning of this chapter, it's best to focus on acting, not on organizing. Limit your management of emails to the bare minimum, and focus on the systematic and concise answering of messages. The time you will save on unnecessary management can be spent doing things you actually like to do with the people you care about.

Mail programs and operating systems are equipped with advanced search functions. Make use of them! Just as in the case of documents and files (see Chapter 7), you can easily find a message from a specific person or concerning a specific topic simply by typing a few characters into the search function. Learn to rely on it, and you'll see that spending hours organizing your emails is simply pointless.

## Email signatures

The aforementioned email signatures (for example, the "Sent from an iPhone" one that my friend uses) can be used so that you don't have to send your regards every time you're sharing the link to your site, blog, profile on a social networking site, and so on. In certain email programs, you can have a few different signatures. I myself have two of them: a private and a business one. The first reads simply "Michael" and the second, "Michael Sliwinski—Founder of Nozbe." You, too, can adapt a footer according to your needs and save some time and energy in the process.

## Standard answers for repetitive questions

Michael Hyatt, a famous blogger and a good friend, once described how he uses email signatures as templates for answers to the most frequently asked questions he receives. He simply reviewed his correspondences and chose around 20 of the questions that he received most often. He prepared the most universal, yet precise, comprehensive, and interesting answers to them. After that, he made them into signatures.

When answering messages containing one of the questions, he would simply choose the proper signature, slightly alter it, and send the message. This way he managed to save himself some time, yet still was able to offer detailed answers to his readers' and fans' questions. Instead of signatures, in other email programs, you can try to use drafts or email templates.

## Turn off automatic notifications

Back in the '90s when electronic mail was a novelty, every new message brought me great joy. These days, there are so many messages that they've become a source of stress rather than glee. This is why I recommend turning off notifications for new emails—both on your computer as well as on your smartphone or tablet. This way, you won't fall into the compulsive habit of always checking your emails after hearing a notification sound and will learn to consciously deal with your emails.

## Set a time to clear out your email inbox

Rather than let yourself be ruled by the automatic notifications that encourage you to constantly look at your email, decide for yourself when to deliberately log in.

- **How?** Always start by checking the newest item and go down the list. By doing so, you avoid reading the same content multiple times. Get to zero, and leave your email inbox. Done.
- **When? How often?** This is a matter of individual preference. However, if you don't work in customer service and don't have to reply to messages all day, you can decide on specific hours during which you can manage your inbox. Some people go in every hour, others schedule time for email.
- **In the morning?** No way! As I've already mentioned in the chapter on priorities (Chapter 3), I never check my email in the morning. I do, however, focus on my three key tasks for the day. It's only around noon that I manage my newly received messages, trying to zero my email folder. Afterward, I log in to it a few more times and manage my emails on the fly.
- **Less than once a day?** Why not? Of course, frequency is an individual matter. Some people check their inbox twice a day, others do it only on specific days of the week. It's all up to you. It depends on your work methods as well as the role that emails play in your private and professional life. Try out different patterns of frequency, different techniques, and decide which methods will bring you closer to realizing your goals.

Regarding "morning email," Csaba, one of our Nozbe users, had this to add:

*"I do think that NOT checking email in the morning is the single most important factor of productivity. Although there is no consensus in productivity literature on whether it is a must or not, it will bring joy into your day and by completing one to three important tasks early in the day, before anybody hits the office, you feel satisfied even if the rest of the day does not work according to your plans. It is, however, not easy to resist checking your emails, so it is best not to open your email in the morning. You are likely to receive negative questions from your colleagues like, "Didn't you receive my email I sent late last night?" Feel free to let them know that your morning is sacred, and you won't let others govern your morning routine."*

Claire, a book launch team member and a Nozbe user, adds another great tip on using "email autoresponders" as a way to inform people that you might not answer their email right away:

*"One thing I've tried is to set up an auto-reply (like an out of office message) just for internal users when I am going to be away from email for a large block of time on a specific day. 'I will be focusing on an important project until (insert*

*time) and will not be checking email. If an urgent matter arises, please contact (insert either a cell number or an assistant's contact info).' This sets expectations with others and helps me resist the urge for a quick peek at my inbox because I know if there's a true emergency, I will be contacted in another way."*

## Don't read the same message twice

I've already written about this above, but it needs repeating: When opening your email, make immediate decisions. If a message requires action, export it to your task list. If it contains a document, decide what to do with it and do it. If you no longer want to receive messages from a source, set up a filter or unsubscribe from it. This way, you'll clean up your email's inbox faster. Don't read the same message twice unless it gives you pleasure!

## Use a good application for working with emails

There are many good applications on the market for managing emails—not only the ones that are already on our operating system but also ones on the internet as well as apps for smartphones and tablets. Many of them come equipped with interesting functions, such as "gestures" that allow you to use different motions of your fingers to quickly export or delete messages as well as many other clever ways of dealing with the incoming flood of messages. It's worth taking a look and trying some of them out. I'm sure you'll find something that suits you. We've added links to a bunch of them in the bonus materials to this chapter.

## Come up with a good channel of communication for your team

As I've already mentioned in Chapter 5 on cooperation, it's worth considering whether or not you'll be communicating with your team using email. Perhaps it would be better to create your own channel of communication, so that important messages wouldn't get mixed up with emails from strangers.

In my company, we communicate using tasks within shared projects in Nozbe, and we use additional apps for chatting, video-calling, and documentation. This way, we manage to clearly separate communication within the company and communication with clients, contractors, and the rest of the world. This kind of divide considerably reduces the number of incoming messages and shortens the time necessary for managing emails. Communication within the team is uninterrupted by notifications from social networks and promotional emails.

Furthermore, communicating through comments in tasks is more effective and brings us all closer to getting them done, and consequently helps us achieve our goals and successfully complete our projects.

# **Exercise:** Your way of dealing with email

1. On what devices do you access your email inbox?

_____

2. Do you have your email notifications turned on?

⚪ Yes     ⚪ No

3. Do you have fixed hours for processing your emails?

⚪ If yes, what are they? _____

⚪ If no, how often do you check your inbox? _____

4. Which tips from this chapter will you apply to improve the way you deal with incoming emails?

_____

_____

_____

5. What other ideas do you have to improve it?

_____

_____

_____

## Chapter 9 Action Plan: Take control of your emails better than ever

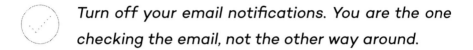 *Turn off your email notifications. You are the one checking the email, not the other way around.*

*Decide on specific times for processing emails. Clean out your inbox every day, using the Two-Minute Rule and other tips from this chapter by immediately deciding what to do with each message.*

*Make sure that an excess of messages doesn't demotivate you from clearing your inbox. Limit the number of received newsletters by unsubscribing from the ones that no longer interest you.*

*Consider changing the method of communication within your team from emails to a more task--oriented form of communication. More on that in Chapter 5 and in the bonus materials.*

**Good luck!**

 **Bonus materials:** If you want even more information on the effective handling of emails, download a package of practical articles, templates, and videos that I've prepared for you today. **ProductivityCourse.com/bonus**

In this chapter, you will learn these basic time management techniques:

→ **The Pomodoro Technique**

⟶ **The Unscheduled Calendar**

⟶ **Your accountability partner**

⟶ **Exercising and reading books—at the same time!**

⟶ **Touch-typing**

→ **Let yourself be inspired!**

⟶ **Read more books on productivity**

⟶ **Start today!**

# **Step 10.** What Else Can You Improve?

*How to supercharge your productivity—some more advanced techniques*

In this final chapter, you will learn some additional tips that can improve your efficiency even more.

## How to effectively manage your off days

In Chapter 3, I recommend determining the three most important tasks for the day and beginning your work day by completing at least one of them. However, time stops for no one, and often things that should take a few minutes end up taking me several hours. Other times, despite trying to focus, the day just feels out of control, and I can't get myself to work on these important tasks. In these situations, I resort to the Pomodoro Technique.

## The Pomodoro Technique

Francesco Cirillo, the creator of this popular technique, was inspired by a kitchen timer in the shape of a tomato (*pomodoro* in Italian). The method involves dividing a day into 30-minute blocks, with 25 of those minutes dedicated to full concentration on work and five minutes dedicated to relaxation. The Pomodoro Technique is most effective in conjunction with a timer that displays each passing minute.

This method helps me not lose track of my concentration. When the clock is ticking, and I am fully aware that I only have 25 minutes to complete my task, I simply start doing it. It keeps me aware of the time passing by and reminds me that I don't have time to be distracted or to do anything on the side; I have to focus on the task at hand. You'd be surprised how much you can accomplish in 25 minutes of full concentration!

Pomodoro also helps me return to my "working mode" on those so-called off days, when I slack off and feel like my mind is trying hard to avoid doing my planned activities. I choose a task, set the timer, the clock starts ticking, and this trick forces me to "just do it." It really works!

If you, too, want to measure your time, you don't need to use a kitchen timer—any kind of timer will do! There are countless computer and phone apps that can also help you with this; you can find links to them in the bonus material for this chapter.

## The Unscheduled Calendar

The Pomodoro Technique can be used very well with a concept of "Unscheduled Calendar," described by Neil Fiore in his book, *The Now Habit*.

The idea is that in your calendar you should schedule everything you want to do apart from work that you have to do. This runs contrary to how we usually view our calendars, but it works like magic. The key to the Unschedule concept is that you do not schedule work on projects.

Instead, you work on your projects in between the times you have scheduled for the activities you want to do.

What you do is put in your calendar only things that must happen—like meetings or meal times—and things you want to do—like sports, playing with kids, reading books, personal time, etc. This allows you to indulge in guilt-free play and enjoy your personal time. When you see how few blocks of work time you really have in between your events, it helps you focus on your work.

For instance, my Unscheduled plan for today looks like this:

- **9:00 a.m. to 9:30 a.m.:** breakfast
- **10:30 a.m. to 12:00 p.m.:** meeting with team leaders of my company
- **3:00 p.m. to 4:30 p.m.:** swimming session.

Now, when you look at it, you can see that I have an hour (9:30 a.m. to 10:30 a.m.) of work between breakfast and the meeting, and three hours (12:00 p.m. to 3:00 p.m.) of work between my meeting and my swimming session (my reward). Now I know I only have these

three hours (or six "pomodoros") between my meeting and my swimming, so I better make them count! I really want to "deserve" my swimming session, and I want this to be my reward for a good day's work.

To keep myself accountable, I also write down what I've done after each half-hour session. Right now, as I am writing these words, it is 12:51 p.m., and in a few minutes, I will enter "writing Step 10 of the book" into the "12:30 p.m. to 1:00 p.m." block. Thanks to this entry, I will know that I still have two hours before my training.

I have prepared a printable template for an Unschedule you can use, as well as one for Nozbe.how, if you prefer a digital version. You can find them in the bonus materials at the end of this chapter.

## Your accountability partner

Team up with someone who is also starting to create their own productivity system, just like you. Work together, share ideas with each other, encourage yourselves to improve your systems, and exchange tips and tricks that you've discovered. Keep track of what you've done—for instance, whether and when you've done your weekly review. You can even do your reviews simultaneously, checking in on each other's progress.

Working in tandem really works! A few years ago, I was overweight and could not motivate myself to go running. I would jog every once in a while, but I would constantly come up with excuses or be preoccupied with something else. My neighbor then came to the rescue and suggested that we start running together once a week. I agreed, so every Tuesday at 9 a.m., after dropping the kids off at school, we would set off on our route. This changed my life. I knew that even if I "wouldn't have the time" during the rest of the week, I would at least be getting exercise once a week.

We gradually began to run more and more; two years later, I went on a diet and allotted myself extra time for swimming and cycling. Now, I regularly participate in triathlons, I'm 22 pounds (10 kilos) lighter, and I feel better than ever. As for my friend, he has taken part in marathons and half-marathons, and this year we plan to take part in at least one running event together. And of course, we still run together on Tuesdays, keeping each other motivated. The support of a second person really helps. For these purposes, you can register for a Nozbe account to create your own shared project, as was outlined in Chapter 5.

## Exercise and read more books—at the same time!

I'd always wanted to read more books, but I kept on telling myself that I didn't have the time. Just like with exercising, I "forced myself" to read, thanks to the help of a friend. I realized that while running alone, I could be doing more. My friend convinced me to listen to podcasts rather than music, after which it occurred to me that I could also be listening to something else—books!

And that was how my audiobook adventure began. In 2009, I had read only two books, while in 2010 that number had skyrocketed to 20! Though, technically, I wasn't actually the one who read them—the narrators did. I listened to books during walks, runs, car rides, train rides, cycling, and even skiing (while riding the cable car)—in other words, in situations that did not require a lot of attention. I now "read" between 20 and 30 books a year.

Thanks to audiobooks, my motivation to do sports has essentially doubled. After all, I no longer go out to just simply run anymore, I also go out to read. Crazy, right?

## Learn touch typing

If you do not yet know how, learn to type without looking at your keyboard. I know that it isn't easy and can feel like I'm sending you back to elementary school. However, after a month you will be able to type not just 20% or 30% faster, but 300% faster!

I had always been a relatively fast typist, but when I tested myself, it turned out that I was typing about 20 to 25 words per minute. Now that I can touch type, I can easily reach 60 words per minute, and in a pinch, I can even reach up to 80. There are even some people who can easily surpass over 100 words!

Consider how much more efficiently you will work when you can respond to emails up to three times faster. Things that used to take you half an hour suddenly become 10-minute tasks. Learning touch typing is an investment that will pay off for many years. There are many courses available, both free and paid, that will help you master this skill. You'll find links to apps and courses I recommend in the bonus materials to this chapter.

## Let yourself be inspired!

I hope that this book will motivate you to further improve your productivity system. My goal here is to help you develop new habits that will not only increase your efficiency, but also help you in finding a sense of balance in your personal and professional life.

## Read more books about productivity

I encourage you to dig deeper into the methods and techniques of productivity. Some authors I would recommend include David Allen, Stephen Covey, Tim Ferriss, Greg McKeown, Charles Duhigg, and Laura Stack. I've attached a full list of names and books to the bonus materials for this chapter. I also recommend the *Productive! Magazine* archive in which you will find articles written by experts in the fields of productivity and personal development, and get to know the people who inspire me. Each issue features a comprehensive interview.

You can also read blogs on productivity and personal development. We publish plenty of practical resources on our Nozbe blog. I also recommend reading entries on websites such as michaelhyatt.com, robbymiles.com, and zenhabits.net.

## Start today!

Complete the activities from the end of each chapter of this book. Start by familiarizing yourself with the Two-Minute Rule and methods for clearing your mind, then continue introducing the next techniques for boosting your productivity.

## Here's the summary of this book in just one paragraph

Start building your productivity system: Add new tasks and projects (Step 1), move tasks and any other materials to appropriate projects and lists (Step 2), delete unnecessary information, and define which tasks you should work on next (Step 3). Set up your system on all of your devices (Step 4). See if you can share any of your projects—just figure out who can help you accomplish your goals (Step 5). Try to tweak your system to make it more action-oriented by categorizing some of your tasks (Step 6). Attach some documents to the tasks that require them (Step 7). Work this way for a week and you'll start seeing the first results. After that, do a weekly review (Step 8). Take a look at your inbox view, check each project and sort them, adding any missing tasks. Start your email routine by choosing times for your email processing (Step 9). You should also think about what can be improved upon or changed. Keep on getting better (Step 10).

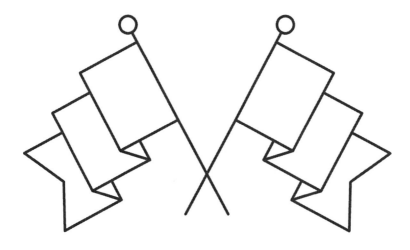

I encourage you to return to this book after a week. Maybe you'll notice something that you had previously missed that could help you further improve your system. Next, set up a date for your next review. Continue this routine, and don't skip your weekly meetings with yourself.

Lastly, check out the bonus materials. At the end of each chapter, I've included a link to bonus packages, where you can find many articles, tutorial videos, and other resources that could prove to be useful for you. Download them to your computer, or import them to your Nozbe account.

# **Exercise:** put some tips into practice

### 1. Plan your ideal day

Use the practical planner template you will find in the bonus materials of this chapter, or start writing right here:

| | From | To | Number of "pomodoros" (30 minutes) |
|---|---|---|---|
| | | | |
| | | | |
| | | | |
| | | | |
| | | | |
| | | | |
| | | | |

## 2. Choose your accountability partner

Think of someone who would like to get better organized and to join you in implementing new productivity techniques.

## 3. Get inspired

What books and blog posts will you read this month?

What podcasts and audiobooks will you listen to?

## 4. Touch typing

Check out **the bonus materials** from this chapter for the list of apps and tests. See what score you get. If it turns out to be disappointing, decide:

• Which app will you use to improve your typing?

• How many minutes per day will you practice?

• What time will you start your touch-typing lesson every day?

## Let's get to work!

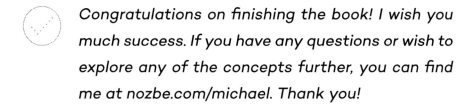

*Congratulations on finishing the book! I wish you much success. If you have any questions or wish to explore any of the concepts further, you can find me at nozbe.com/michael. Thank you!*

*Do the activities and exercises at the end of each chapter of this book.*

*Download the accompanying bonus materials and learn from them. Set aside some time to look through the material that you think would be most useful to you.*

*Recommend this book to your friends. Along with the publishing team, we at Nozbe have put a lot of work, energy, and money into it. We would like it to help as many people as possible.*

**Thanks!**

**Bonus materials:** If you want to discover even more ways of increasing your productivity and get one extra month of Nozbe, check out a package of practical articles, templates, and videos that will help motivate you to get moving and organize your life. **ProductivityCourse.com/bonus**

# Final Productivity Problems & Solutions

---

I'm sure that by the time you finish reading this book, you may have quite a few questions. Make sure to send them my way, or post them in our "Ultimate Productivity" Facebook group. Here are a few of the issues that tend to keep coming back; see if you can relate:

## 1. I'm constantly failing to carry out my planned tasks.

Perhaps your current working style isn't the one for you. Maybe you should simply start by listing what you have to do and what you cannot afford to forget about. Identify your priority tasks and how long it will take to complete them. If they are complex, break them up into smaller steps. Carry the list with you and make sure to look at it from time to time. Remember that these are things that you must do! After some time, you'll get the hang of it.

## 2. For some strange reason, I keep on avoiding my weekly reviews.

The human mind is a clever beast and will protect itself from any form of exertion. It associates your task list with work, which is why it discourages you from conducting reviews. It keeps whispering, not now, maybe later, soon, tomorrow, you must first clean the apartment until it shines, etc. You must remember that you are the only one who can stand up to it. Hang the list somewhere visible or always have it with you. This way, it will be hard for you to not look at it. You can also use phone reminders or other tools.

Remember, this is one of your most important meetings. If you attend it, you will gain more clarity and control over your schedule, all the tasks on your plate, and the habits you care about. It will keep you in balance and that is exactly what you may need in your busy life!

One particular hack I find useful (and described in Chapter 8) is to change contexts; go to a café, conference room, or somewhere else and force yourself not to leave the place until the review is done. It works for me! Hello, Starbucks!

### 3. I've forgotten my paper or notebook with my tasks.

To avoid forgetting your materials, save tasks in a way that allows you to have access to the list no matter the time or place. I advise using a document in the cloud or a dedicated application that synchronizes automatically and works on many devices. This way, all you'll need is a computer or phone with internet access, and the problem is solved. As I explained in Chapter 4, we live in the 21st century; it's time to embrace the cloud and the internet. Paper doesn't sync with anything!

### 4. I have a task that I keep postponing. I'm having trouble getting it started.

Perhaps your task has been defined too broadly. Maybe you should try making it more precise or break it up into smaller steps, turning the task into a small project. As humans, we tend to get a rush after checking something off of our list; we get a sense of completion. The moment you tick off one thing that you've finished motivates you to do more! Another hack I have found useful is setting aside a full two-hour block to get a hard task done. I was trying to finish this book and kept postponing editing the last two chapters, but when I finally set aside a full two-hour block; I finished it off! So happy!

### 5. I planned out a few tasks for the day, but I wasn't able to even begin working on most of

**them. This happens quite often. I make plans and do one, maybe two of the tasks, but sometimes I don't finish even a single one.**

When formulating tasks, consider how much time you think you'll need to finish them. Try overestimating the amount of time each task will take rather than under-estimating. Remember, there are only 24 hours in a day. So, designate some time to work on the tasks (maybe four hours a day), decide how much time you'll need for each of them individually, and start acting. Remember the importance of setting priorities for your tasks. Learn to distinguish the difference between what's important and what's not. It's also useful NOT to check email or so-cial media in the morning. Start your day with the tasks that are important to you and to you only!

**6. I'm sick, I've broken my arm, my child has chicken pox, etc. There is no way for me to do my tasks. The list is getting longer, and the deadlines are slipping by.**

Some things can't be helped. What's most important is to keep calm. With time, you'll get everything back in order. If you have the option, ask someone to help you out. Have them go through your list with you and help you reorganize it. Perhaps they could even take care of some smaller mat-ters for you. Maybe you'll even come to the decision that sometimes it's best to delegate your tasks to those who are able to get them done better than you can. It's worth trying.

## 7. Since I've moved everything into my own system, I'm having a harder time remembering my tasks and deadlines.

This is rather normal. After all, you have a clear mind! Your mind is now also open to new ideas, which you should make sure to put into good use. Now you need to count on your calendar and your system to remind you about things—and that's how it's supposed to work! Make sure to always have either a notebook with a pen, or a smartphone with an application for taking notes with you. Perform regular reviews as well, and you'll see that with time your brain will get used to operating this way. You'll be all the more satisfied when you start tackling the tasks you've written down and effectively checking them off your list, not off your mind.

## 8. I'm an organized and productive person. I'd like to help out my family and friends, and convince them to manage their time and tasks more efficiently.

It's simple. Recommend this book to your loved ones! It's also important to demonstrate the value of these techniques by setting a good example. And you're one of them! Show them your system. Show them the perks of planning and creating tasks. Tell them how your life has changed the moment you started to effectively manage your tasks. Many of our readers have said that instead of telling someone, "you better get organized," they simply handed them this book and told them, "check out this short book, you might find it useful."

# Final Thoughts

Wow! You've just finished a book with tips and advice necessary to help you take your first 10 steps towards maximum productivity. Since you've still got work ahead of you—putting this newly acquired knowledge into practice—I'm keeping my fingers crossed for you! I can't wait to hear what you'll accomplish now. Let me know via social media—tag me in a post; I love hearing from my readers!

The ultimate productivity that I've mentioned in every chapter isn't some deadly grind but a lifestyle—an approach that assumes rational planning; well-organized, effective action; and systematic development.

The result is a harmonious sense of control and fulfillment, as well as time that we can spend with our loved ones or pursuing our passions.

Many people have already made use of my course and are living proof of its effectiveness. Why not further expand this group of happy, well-organized people? Give your friends or coworkers a hand, help them face the flood of responsibilities and stress—recommend this book to them. It was made to be shared!

# Acknowledgments

Thank you for finding the time to read my book. I hope that the lessons I prepared will help you become more efficient. I am certain you will soon see for yourself that greater productivity leads to greater happiness in life! From the bottom of my heart, I extend my thanks to everyone who helped in creating, promoting, and distributing this publication, namely the most active members of the publishing team:

Aiko Yao Lim, Alessio Rozzi, Anabell Perales, Andrea Sloan, Angela Weekes, Anne McDonley, Barbara Hopkins, Bee Kiong Kang, Bill Johnson, Catherine Wynne-Paton, Chad Garrett, Charles Olsen, Chuck Burks, Claire Kellems, Csaba Vadadi-Fulop, Dale Lepine, Daniel Wintersdorf, Danny Tobon, Darla S. Grieco, David Fiene, Douglas White, Ed Roden, Eric Ekong, Eric Putnam, Gary Mintchell, Gina Wolf, Greg Phelan, Gus, Heather Berube, Ian Hunter, James Nixon, John Wright, Jolanda ter Maten, JP O'Sullivan, Juha Rantakari, Kacy Burns, Kristóf Eszes, Lexi Mitchell, Melvin Whartnaby, Michael Bartura, Michael Crook, Michael Kamutzki, Michele Wiedemer, Mike St. Pierre, Piotr Zagorowski, Ralph Broadwater, Renee Kresl, Robby Miles, Robert A. Lopez, Rodney Weikel, Ryan Salvanera, Ryan Stewart, Samantha A. Johnston, Sanjay Prabhu, Tim Fus, Trish Rempel, W. Patrick Jones and Wes Ory.